m

tips and techniques

AN A-Z GUIDE

microwave
tips and techniques

AN A-Z GUIDE

PENGUIN BOOKS

Penguin Books Australia Ltd
487 Maroondah Highway, PO Box 257
Ringwood, Victoria 3134, Australia
Penguin Books Ltd
Harmondsworth, Middlesex, England
Viking Penguin, A Division of Penguin Books USA Inc.
375 Hudson Street, New York, New York 10014, USA
Penguin Books Canada Limited
10 Alcorn Avenue, Toronto, Ontario, Canada M4V 3B2
Penguin Books (N.Z.) Ltd
182–190 Wairau Road, Auckland 10, New Zealand

First published by Penguin Books Australia, 1992
Revised edition published by Penguin Books Australia 1995
10 9 8 7 6 5 4 3 2 1

Typeset by Post Typesetters, Queensland
Printed in Australia by Australian Print Group, Victoria

National Library of Australia
Cataloguing-in-Publication data

Microwave tips and techniques.

Updated and rev. ed.

ISBN 0 14 025349 1.

1. Microwave cookery.

641.5882

CONTENTS

INTRODUCTION

The microwave oven has, in a very short time, become a standard piece of equipment in the kitchen. Its place is deserved: it is an extremely fast, convenient, clean and inexpensive way to cook. However, because microwave ovens work in a completely different way from conventional ovens, new techniques have to be used when cooking with them.

When you first acquire a microwave oven, it's really worthwhile familiarising yourself with all these new techniques. It isn't difficult, but you have to think about what you are cooking in a slightly different way. Try to attend an introductory class in microwave cookery and begin by cooking basic dishes until you gain confidence.

In microwave cooking a power level has to be set on the oven, instead of a temperature. Timing is extremely important, too, for the length of time a dish will take to cook will depend on the amount, shape, density and moisture content of the ingredients. Overcooking is the most common mistake made by those new to microwave cookery, so don't guess cooking times. Follow the recipe's timings, and remember that foods continue to cook during the prescribed standing time given in many recipes.

Most recipes are for ovens with a wattage of 600–700 watts. Older, smaller ovens may be less powerful – 500 watts or so – while there are newer ovens on the market of 1000 watts. To cook successfully with your microwave you *must* know its wattage. A less powerful oven than average will mean cooking times will be *longer* than those given in recipes (and in this book). A more powerful oven will mean *shorter* cooking times, although you also have the option of setting a lower power level than suggested in the recipe. When in doubt check the cooking early on, as you can always put a dish back in the oven if it is not ready but there is no remedy for overcooking.

The equipment and utensils for microwave cooking may differ from your conventional ones. Metal, including gold-edged dishes, must not be used in the microwave oven, and you may find you have to buy some equipment. Look for the 'microwave safe' label on anything you purchase.

With a little practice you will find the convenience of the microwave oven will transform your cooking habits, and the hints and techniques in this book will facilitate your mastery of the microwave.

A–Z

A

Absorption of microwaves
☐ Microwaves are absorbed by food and penetrate about 1–4 cm deep. The microwave energy works on the molecules in the food (especially water, fat and sugar molecules) and makes them vibrate 2,450,000,000 times per second. This vibration produces the heat that cooks the food.

Adapting recipes see Converting recipes

Almonds
☐ Almonds can be toasted in your microwave oven by placing on a glass dish; for 200 g, microwave on HIGH (100%) for 4–6 minutes, stirring several times.

Aluminium foil see also Shielding
☐ Aluminium foil is the only metal that *can* be used in microwave ovens. As microwaves cannot penetrate the foil, we use foil to protect food such as chicken wings or the end of a leg of lamb from overcooking during the cooking or defrosting cycle.
☐ Foil must be at least 2.5 cm away from the oven lining and door.
☐ When shielding, always:
   - check the handbook instructions
   - use wooden toothpicks to hold foil in place if necessary
   - use small, smooth pieces of foil.

☐ Don't cover more than a third of whatever you are cooking with foil.

☐ If arcing (blue sparks) occurs, rearrange the foil. If arcing continues remove the foil.

☐ Shielding with foil helps in much microwave cooking.

☐ **Poultry:** protect chicken legs, wing tips and breast meat on larger birds.

☐ **Lamb:** cover the bony ends of joints to prevent overcooking.

☐ **Fish:** protect areas easily overcooked, such as heads and tails.

☐ **Bread and cakes:** if cooking in square containers the corners can overcook, so shield the corners.

☐ Aluminium foil is very useful when defrosting. Shield outer, warm areas so they do not begin to cook before the rest of the food is defrosted.

☐ Food can be wrapped in foil for freezing. Microwaving and freezing go well together.

☐ Aluminium trays can be used if they are very shallow (no deeper than 2.5 cm) and do not touch the sides of the oven. Remember to remove the lid. The microwaves will penetrate only from the top, so food in an aluminium tray will take longer to cook or heat than if it were in a glass or plastic container. Foil trays can come straight from the freezer to the microwave once the lid is off.

Appetisers see also **Dips**

☐ To serve a dip warm, you can spread it on a cracker and heat for 10 seconds in the microwave on HIGH (100%).

☐ Individual small items, such as canapes, mushrooms, meatballs and tiny frankfurts, are best and most evenly cooked if they're placed around the edge of the turntable plate. Remember always to pierce frankfurts before cooking.

☐ Dishwashing is an unwelcome adjunct to entertaining;. Place appetisers on paper towels, paper plates or napkins for easy clearing up.

☐ Freeze dips and appetisers, then defrost and heat just before entertaining. Don't exhaust yourself on the day. Cook when you have time.

Apples

☐ Apples can be stewed in their skins to retain more flavour and vitamins. Pierce the apple's skin, place in the microwave and heat on HIGH (100%) for 2 minutes to bake the apple, 3 minutes for stewed apple. Once cooked, it is easy to remove the skin and the apple will keep its colour during cooking.

Arcing

☐ Arcing is when small sparks appear in the oven, accompanied by a clicking noise. It is caused by metal in the oven, that should not be there, or by aluminium foil touching the metal lining, or damage to the oven's lining, such as scratches from cleaning. Take out the offending dish (check plates for metal trim, and remember some mugs and cups have metal-reinforced handles) or rearrange foil. Arcing won't damage if quickly rectified.

Arranging food in oven see also **Placement**

☐ As microwaves work from the outside, food at the outer edges of a container will cook more quickly than food in the centre. Therefore thicker or denser pieces of food should always be at the outside of the turntable or dish.

☐ When cooking similarly sized pieces of food, such as rolls, small cakes, potatoes or apples, arrange them in a circle around the edge of the turntable, with about 2.5 cm between each.

☐ Some microwave ovens have 'cold' spots towards the centre, so avoid putting a dish here.

☐ Small pieces of food, such as peas or carrots, should be placed as evenly as possible in the dish rather than piled up in the middle.

☐ If your oven does not have a turntable, you will have to turn the dish 3–4 times during cooking.

☐ For plate meals, place thin foods such as sliced meat in the middle of the plate and keep the hard-fibred vegetables arranged evenly around.

Artichoke (globe)

☐ To prepare for microwaving, if possible soak for 15–20 minutes to soften. Pull off the coarse, outer leaves, trim remaining leaves and base of artichoke. Rinse and drain. Brush with lemon juice. Place in a plastic freezer or oven bag and secure with a string or elastic band.

☐ Microwave 1 artichoke for approximately 2–4 minutes on HIGH (100%); 2 artichokes for 5–8 minutes. Serve with vinaigrette or Hollandaise sauce, or melted butter.

Asparagus

- [ ] To cook, trim and peel base of stalks. Place on platter with tips towards the centre. Sprinkle with a few drops of water, cover with plastic wrap. Cook on HIGH (100%); 250 g will take 2–4 minutes.
- [ ] Always peel asparagus with a potato peeler for best results in the microwave.
- [ ] If cooking in a bunch, wrap the tips in foil to prevent over-cooking before the stalks are tender.

Aspic

- [ ] When preparing food in aspic, use the microwave to help dissolve the aspic powder in water. If the jelly is difficult to work with while coating, microwave on HIGH (100%) for 20–30 seconds to soften.

Avocado

- [ ] You can ripen avocados in the microwave by heating them for up to 2 minutes on LOW (10%), turning once during the heating time. Be careful not to overdo it or the avocado will start to blacken inside.

B

Babies' bottles and food

- [ ] Baby milk in glass bottles (plastic is not recommended) and food can safely be reheated in the microwave if the correct timing is used.

☐ Always remove the teat before heating.
☐ Always reheat on MEDIUM (50–60%) to prevent too rapid a rise in temperature. Remember reheating will only take seconds: a bottle of 240 ml will take about 50 seconds on MEDIUM to reach blood temperature from refrigerator temperature.
☐ It is far safer for the feed to be too cold than too hot.
☐ Never feed straight from the microwave. Always allow standing time as heating will continue after the oven has stopped. Then always thoroughly *shake* the milk or *stir* the food to ensure the heat is distributed evenly, and test it yourself to check the feed is not too hot.
☐ Sterilising feeding bottles and teats in a microwave is *not* recommended.
☐ For safest results put milk in a Pyrex jug and transfer to the baby's bottle.

Bacon
☐ To cook crisp, fat-free slices of bacon, and have no washing up, snip the rind and place the bacon between several pieces of paper towel. Cook for about 1 minute per slice on HIGH (100%), then let stand for 1 minute.
☐ Streaky bacon will take slightly less time to cook than back bacon.
☐ To separate uncooked bacon slices, place packet in microwave and defrost on MEDIUM-LOW (30%) for 1–2 minutes. Allow to stand for 3 minutes and you will then be able to peel off slices of bacon without tearing them.
☐ Bacon for barbecue or a crowd: you can microwave 50 slices

or more the day before, lay them out on paper towels, cover and then refrigerate. Reheat on HIGH (100%) in the paper towels just long enough to heat well and regain the crispness.

Bags *see* **Cooking bags, Paper, Plastic**

Baked custard

☐ Always start with ingredients at room temperature. You can warm the milk and cream in the microwave using DEFROST (30%) for 30 seconds.

☐ Overcooked custard is tough and separates. Always take from microwave when just set and still a little soft in the centre. Standing time will complete the cooking.

☐ When completely cooked, a knife should come out clean when inserted about 2.5 cm from the centre of the custard.

☐ If not quite set, return to the oven and cook on MEDIUM (50–60%) for a few minutes.

Banana

☐ For a very quick snack, cook a firm banana in its skin on HIGH (100%) for 1 minute. Serve with ice-cream and cinnamon.

Baskets

☐ Baskets can be used for quick reheating of food such as rolls. Don't use glued baskets as the glue could melt, or baskets wired or stapled together. If baskets are left in the microwave for a long time, they can dry out.

Bay leaves

☐ Bay leaves should be crumbled finely just before they are used so that they will release more flavour.

Beans
- [ ] **Broad beans**: to cook fresh broad beans, place in a small, covered dish with 2 tablespoons of water. Cook on HIGH (100%): 250 g will take 5–6 minutes.
- [ ] To cook frozen broad beans, microwave from frozen on HIGH in a covered microwave dish. Stir twice during cooking. A 375 g pack will take 7–8 minutes.
- [ ] If you are having problems cooking broad beans or lima beans, remember they are hard-fibred, so try a little more water, add no salt and cover the dish tightly. Just because they are green doesn't mean their fibres are soft.
- [ ] **French beans**: to cook fresh French beans, trim and slice thinly lengthwise. Rinse and place in a plastic freezer bag and secure. Cook on HIGH (100%); 500 g will take 5–6 minutes.
- [ ] To cook frozen French beans, place in a small covered dish with a knob of butter or margarine and cook on HIGH (100%); 150 g will take 2–4 minutes.
- [ ] If you want to cook French beans whole, arrange them on a plate like the spokes of a wheel, sprinkle with a few drops of water and cover with plastic wrap.

Beef see also **Casseroles, Meat, Roasting, Steak**
- [ ] To cook a joint of beef on the bone, microwave for 10–12 minutes per 500 g on MEDIUM (50–60%) for a rare result; 12–15 minutes per 500 g on MEDIUM (50–60%) for a medium result and 15–18 minutes per 500 g on MEDIUM (50–60%) for well done. Allow meat to stand covered with foil for 10–15 minutes.
- [ ] To cook a joint of beef such as topside or fillet, microwave for

12–15 minutes per 500 g on MEDIUM (50–60%) for a rare result; 15–18 minutes per 500 g on MEDIUM (50–60%) for a medium result and 18–20 minutes per 500 g on MEDIUM (50–60%) for a well-done result. Allow meat to stand covered with foil for 10–15 minutes.

☐ It is essential that the meat be of good quality to cook successfully in the microwave.

Beetroot

☐ To cook 4 medium beetroots, about 500 g, cut into cubes. Place in covered dish with ¼ cup water and cook on HIGH (100%) for 10–12 minutes.

Biscuits

☐ Biscuits are tricky in a microwave – bar-type biscuits are more successful than drop biscuits, which cook very quickly, tend to crumble, and burn very easily in the centre. For large quantities of biscuits use your conventional oven because microwave results are poor. But experimenting is worthwhile. Next time you bake biscuits conventionally, test a few in the microwave oven to see how well that particular recipe works.

☐ Follow recipes that have been specially developed for cooking in the microwave. You will be much happier with the results.

☐ Chill the biscuit dough before baking. Cook chilled biscuits until there are no doughy spots. If biscuits are over-baked brown spots will appear in the middle. Allow biscuits to cool and harden on tray before removing.

☐ Putting a piece of cardboard on the turntable helps to get a good result with biscuits.

☐ Biscuit batters you are going to cook in a dish and then slice are best done in a 30 cm x 20 cm dish on MEDIUM (50–60%) for 8–10 minutes. Cut into squares when cool. Do not cover while microwaving – a cover helps keep the moisture in. Use foil to cover the corners of a square baking dish to prevent over-cooking the edges.

☐ Soggy biscuits? Revive them on HIGH (100%) for 45–60 seconds, then let them stand for a few minutes and they will crisp.

Blanching

☐ If lots of vegetables are to be blanched conventional blanching will be easier.

☐ For small amounts microwave blanching is ideal as it retains more nutrients (especially Vitamin C), which are normally lost in water blanching.

Prepare vegetables in the usual way. Work out how long they would take to cook in the microwave. Blanching will take *half* this time. Microwave in a freezer bag. Then plunge immediately into ice-cold water to cool, drain, pack and freeze.

Bones see also **Soup, Stock**

☐ You can freeze leftover bones from joints and defrost them in your microwave when you need a good stock or soup.

Books

☐ Try to buy Australian microwave cookery books, as imported books may not have correct timings for recipes, because the electrical power input can be different overseas from the Australian standard.

☐ Check the copyright date before you buy a microwave cook book – books printed before 1980 frequently don't include power variables, so you will find their recipes restricted compared with newer books.

☐ Microwave ovens have increased in output power since 1990. The most common microwaves now between 750 and 900 watts. Therefore if you have replaced your old microwave with a new one in the last five years you will find your old microwave recipes will not take quite as long to cook. Try reducing the power level – it is easier than guessing the cooking time.

Bottles
☐ Reheat babies' glass bottles for 30 seconds on MEDIUM (50–60%) to get to the right temperature. Reheating feeds in plastic bottles is not recommended.

Brandy
☐ Be very careful when warming brandy or liqueurs in your microwave for flambéd desserts. Place 2 tablespoons of the brandy or liqueur in a small, heat-proof bowl or a 250-ml jug, heat on HIGH (100%) for 30–40 seconds, remove from the oven and ignite with a taper. Carefully pour over the dish. As a dessert try ice-cream topped with cherries and flambéd with brandy, or Grand Marnier bananas. For a more spectacular presentation, pour the heated brandy into a large heated ladle and then ignite, but keep well away from any paper napkins or you will have a mini-bonfire!

Bread

☐ You can **prove** dough in the microwave: place it in a greased microwaveable container. Half fill a 2-cup glass jug with water and microwave on HIGH (100%) for 5 minutes or until the oven is filled with steam. Put the dough in the oven. It should double in size in about 45 minutes.

☐ An alternative way to prove dough is to put it in a large container, cover with plastic wrap and put it into the oven. Microwave on LOW (10–20%) for 10–15 minutes.

☐ To **defrost** frozen bread dough fill the microwave with steam as above. Place dough in the oven and microwave on DEFROST (30%) for 7–8 minutes, turning over two or three times. Make sure you don't start to cook the dough. Let it stand 5 minutes before working.

☐ **Microwave bread** is good for soft sandwich bread and for toasting, but will not brown. If you want browned bread, finish cooking in a conventional oven for 5 minutes at 220°C, or slip under the grill for several minutes.

☐ Bread made in the microwave tends to dry out quickly so store it in an airtight container, or wrap in foil in the refrigerator.

☐ Zucchini bread or a nutbread are attractive, easy to make in the microwave and good for slicing and sandwiches.

☐ To **reheat** a loaf of bread, wrap in paper towels and heat on MEDIUM-HIGH (70%) for 1–2 minutes or until just warm. Eat immediately. Don't heat too long – a loaf heated for more than 3 minutes will be rock hard on cooling!

☐ To **reheat bread rolls**: heat on MEDIUM (50%) for only 10–20 seconds per roll.

☐ Stale bread can be refreshed by wrapping in a damp cotton or linen (*not* synthetic) serviette or towel and heating for a few seconds, but you need to eat it warm.

Breadcrumbs

☐ Dried breadcrumbs can be made quickly in the microwave. Scatter 150–200 g bread, cut into cubes, over a paper towel, place on a roasting rack and cook on HIGH (100%) for 2–3 minutes, stirring several times. Cool, then crumble the cubes as required.

Broccoli

☐ To cook 500 g of fresh broccoli, cut into even sized florets, rinse and place in plastic freezer or oven bag. Secure. Microwave on HIGH (100%) for 4–6 minutes.

☐ Frozen broccoli: empty a 375 g pack into a dish with the stems facing towards the outside. Cover. Cook on HIGH (100%) for 4–6 minutes, stirring once.

☐ To avoid any waste, save the stems of broccoli or cauliflower. Peel these with a potato peeler, arrange in a dish or cut into 1-cm slices and cook with the florets, stirring once or twice during cooking. Uncooked stems can also be added to a salad or stew, or create an unusual and colourful garnish.

Brown rice see also **Rice**

☐ To cook brown rice, put 500 ml water and a tablespoon of oil into a microwave-safe dish and heat on HIGH (100%) for 4 minutes. Add 1 cup of brown rice, stir, cover and heat on MEDIUM-HIGH (70%) for 25 minutes. Allow to stand for at least 10 minutes. If this seems rather a long cooking time, remember that it only costs about 10c to run your microwave for 30 minutes, so it is much cheaper to cook this way than on top of the stove.

Brown sugar
☐ To soften brown sugar that has become hard, add a slice of white bread or an apple wedge to 200 g sugar and heat in a covered container for 30–40 seconds on HIGH (100%).

Browning see also Colour, Toppings
☐ Generally foods do not brown naturally while cooking in the microwave. For food to be visually appealing we suggest you marinade or baste meat and poultry.
☐ Meat has to be cooked at a lower power setting to prevent it becoming tough. To ensure a brown colour baste the meat with one of the following: Parisian essence; soy sauce, melted butter and paprika; Worcestershire sauce; melted currant jelly; honey; barbecue sauce; commercial microwave browning agents.
☐ For a brown crust, casseroles can be topped with toasted breadcrumbs, mixed with Parmesan cheese if you wish, after final stirring.
☐ Pastry can be browned by adding a few drops of soy sauce or Worcestershire sauce to the recipe, if it is to be used in a savoury dish such as quiche.
☐ Slices and cakes can be browned by using wholemeal flour instead of white, brown sugar, or by adding cinnamon if this is appropriate to the recipe.

Browning dish
☐ Browning dishes are not available in Australia any longer.

Keep an eye out for a second hand one, as they are great for reheating pastries, pies, pizzas and scones.

☐ The browning dishes designed especially for the microwave oven will sear and brown food in much the same way as a frying pan on top of the stove. Browning dishes have a special coating on the bottom that absorbs microwave energy until the dish reaches 250°C, when the bottom of the dish will glow yellow. Browning dishes should always be preheated, empty, on HIGH (100%). If you have a turntable microwave, the dish should be placed at the edge of the turntable rather than in the centre since less energy hits the centre in this style of microwave.

☐ Larger browning dishes may have a well around the side to catch dripping – these are called grillers. Some even have ridges so that the cooked food will look grilled.

☐ Preheating time varies with each recipe. You can preheat small dishes for 1–6 minutes, large dishes for 1–8 minutes. The dish should absorb the maximum energy before cooking meat or fish. But less energy is necessary for egg dishes and more delicate foods. Once the dish is preheated simply add the food and sear it briefly, turn it over and continue cooking. There is no need to wipe the dish and preheat again after turning as the food is served seared-side up.

☐ A browning dish can be used as an ordinary casserole so long as the bottom of the dish is covered with food.

☐ Browning dishes must not be used in a conventional oven or on top of the stove. Don't cover a browning dish with paper.

Don't place a preheated browning dish on a counter – it will burn the counter.

☐ After preheating lightly grease the browning dish so that food doesn't stick to it. Butter and oil can be added to the browning dish in the same way as to a frying pan.

☐ Clean the browning dish with cream cleaner and a soft cloth. Never scratch the surface.

Browning element

☐ Similar to a grill in a conventional oven, a browning element is built into the top of some microwave ovens. It is used to brown food at the start and end of cooking, or sometimes it can be used during microwave cooking.

Brussels sprouts

☐ To cook fresh Brussels sprouts, cut a cross in the stem, rinse and put in a plastic freezer or oven bag. Secure. Cook on HIGH (100%). 500 g will take 4–6 minutes.

☐ To cook frozen Brussels sprouts, spread them out on a dish, cover, and microwave on HIGH (100%), stirring once. A 375 g pack will take 4–5 minutes.

Burgers see also **Hamburgers**

☐ To cook individual burgers, microwave on HIGH (100%) for 1–2 minutes per burger, with 3–4 minutes standing time to complete cooking.

Burning

☐ Microwaves penetrate about 4 cm into food. With small items, such as biscuits or chocolate, the paths of several microwaves may cross; double cooking occurs at this crossing point, and burning. In conventional cookery food burns on the outside; in microwave cookery burning occurs inside the food.

Burnt dishes

☐ You can clean a dish burnt during conventional cooking by filling it with water, adding 2 tablespoons of baking soda and microwaving on HIGH (100%) for 5–6 minutes. Don't try to clean your cast-iron ware this way, though!

Butter

☐ To soften butter from the refrigerator, heat for 30 seconds on MEDIUM (50%) in a microwave-safe jug. If you wish to melt butter, heat for 1 minute on MEDIUM (50%).

☐ To make clarified butter, melt 240 g on butter in a 500-ml, microwave-safe jug on DEFROST (30–40%) for 2–3 minutes or until it is completely melted and the oil is starting to separate. Stand 3–4 minutes, then remove the foam and slowly pour off the yellow oil and put aside. This will make approximately 160 g.

C

Cabbage

☐ To cook cabbage, shred and rinse it and put it in a plastic freezer bag. Secure. Microwave on HIGH (100%); 500 g will take 4–6 minutes.

☐ To prepare cabbage leaves for cabbage rolls, put a whole head of cabbage in the microwave and heat for 5–10 minutes on HIGH (70%). This will soften the outer layer of leaves sufficiently to enable you to pull them off easily and fill and roll them. If you require more leaves, repeat the process.

Cake ring or loop

☐ The best dish for a microwave cake is a round dish with a hole through the centre, called a cake ring or loop. If you don't have one you can improvise by placing a tumbler in the middle of a microwave-safe pan. For best results it should be about 2 litres capacity. Cakes expand on cooking and some rings available are too small for normal quantities of mixture. Cakes do not generally cook successfully in conventionally-shaped tins in the microwave: the centre remains uncooked when the outside is ready.

Cakes see also **Patty cakes, Slices, Sponges**

☐ Lightly grease or line your microwave cake pans. If you are cooking a heavy chocolate mix, a paper towel can be used at the bottom to absorb excess moisture.

☐ When first making cakes in the microwave, use a packet mix – it's a lot less heartrending to throw out a mix than four or five dollars worth of fruit, nuts, etc.

☐ For best results, all ingredients should be at room temperature.

☐ Mix cakes with a fork, not a beater, so the cake does not end up with large air holes in it. For batter cakes, where you have to use a beater, let the batter stand for 10 minutes before cooking to avoid large air holes in the cake.

☐ Cakes made with self-raising flour are often more successful than those made with plain flour. The reason packet cakes are so light in texture is they use a finer self-raising flour.

☐ Add extra liquid when converting your own cake recipes, for example, increase 120 ml to 180 ml, or the cake will be very dry.

☐ Do not fill the cake pan more than half full. Microwave cakes increase substantially in volume and their texture is a little lighter than conventionally baked cakes.

☐ Chocolate cakes tend to cook a little faster than plain cakes.

☐ If you are making a square cake, shield the corners with pieces of foil to prevent overcooking.

☐ Cakes will not brown as in a conventional oven. If you are going to ice the cake this will not be a problem. Alternatively, choose a recipe with built-in colour, such as a chocolate, coffee, ginger or spice cake, or you can use wholemeal flour and brown sugar in the ingredients.

☐ Rich fruit cakes can be darkened by adding 2 or 3 teaspoons of Parisian or coffee essence to the ingredients.

☐ You can give the sides and base of the cake a good colour by greasing the pan very lightly, then sprinkling toasted coconut or fine breadcrumbs over it before putting the mixture in.

☐ Cakes made with butter and sugar are very easy to overcook as the microwaves are attracted to both butter and sugar.

☐ A cake won't fall if you open and shut the door of your microwave oven during cooking.

☐ Put the cake pan on a roasting rack during cooking so that the bottom of the cake cooks evenly.

☐ A cake is cooked when a skewer pierced into the centre comes out clean. At this point the top of the cake will often look moist or uncooked. It will dry out during standing time, which is essential for cakes.

☐ Don't turn out a microwave cake before it has had at least 10 minutes' standing time.

☐ To help keep microwave cakes fresh, put an apple, cut in half, in the storage container. Microwave cakes tend to dry out faster than conventionally cooked ones, particularly packet mixes. You can add a tablespoon of light oil to the ingredients to make the cake moister, or a teaspoon of glycerine.

☐ It is better to use plastic microware instead of glass to cook a cake, as glass retains heat and will continue to cook the cake after it is removed from the oven.

☐ A frozen cake can be defrosted on MEDIUM-LOW/DEFROST (30–40%) for 4–5 minutes. If correctly defrosted it should be cool and cut easily.

Canapés

☐ Canapés can be made quickly and easily. Spread cheese or pâté on crackers or fairy toast, put a paper doily on the microwave turntable and heat the canapés on the turntable for a few seconds. Then just pick up the turntable and use it as a tray to hand round the canapés.

Capsicum

☐ To make capsicums easier to chop, soften them in the microwave for 45 seconds on HIGH (100%), elevated on a roasting rack.

☐ To cook capsicum, chop as required, rinse and place in plastic freezer or oven bag. Secure. Cook on HIGH (100%): 2 capsicums will take about 6–8 minutes to cook.

Carrot

☐ To cook fresh carrots, clean and chop as desired, put into a plastic freezer or oven bag, secure and cook on HIGH (100%): 500 g will take approximately 4–6 minutes.

☐ To cook frozen carrots, spread on a dish, cover and cook on HIGH (100%), stirring once. A 375 g pack will take 3–5 minutes to cook.

☐ By cooking baby carrots unpeeled you retain all their goodness and flavour.

Casserole dishes

☐ Use as saucepans and for casseroles. A set of three is useful, of capacities about 0.75 litres, 1.25 litres and 2.25 litres.

Casseroles

☐ Casseroles can be difficult: remember that there are several types of fibre in the casserole, plus liquid.

☐ Cut the meat into smaller pieces than you would for a conventionally cooked casserole and ensure they are of uniform size. The resulting casserole will be more tender.

☐ Beat the surface of the meat with a hammer or prick it with a fork to help break up connective tissue.

☐ If vegetables are to be added to the casserole, slice them thinly, pop them on a plate and gently soften in the microwave before adding them to the meat. This will ensure that the meat and vegetables are both cooked at the same time.

☐ Add less liquid than you would normally use. More liquid can be added if necessary, just before the end of cooking time, when you thicken the casserole.

☐ Always thicken casseroles towards the end of microwaving, otherwise the result can be gluey. Add thickening agent, plus extra liquid if necessary, about 5–7 minutes before the end of cooking.

☐ Always stir casseroles well during cooking, bringing the outer ingredients to the centre and the less-cooked centre part to the edge of the dish. This will ensure even cooking.

☐ Save money and time by doubling your quantities and freezing half for another meal.

Cauliflower

☐ To cook fresh cauliflower, separate into florets, rinse and place in plastic freezer or oven bag. Secure. Cook on HIGH (100%): 500 g will take 4–6 minutes.

☐ Cauliflower, broccoli and asparagus will cook evenly if the stems are placed towards the outside of the dish. The stems are tougher than the flower ends and so will benefit from the more concentrated microwaves at the edge of the oven.

Celery

☐ To cook fresh celery, slice thinly, place in a small covered dish and cook on HIGH (100%): 300 g will take 3–4 minutes.

Centres of food cooked first

☐ Sometimes the centre of food gets hot, and perhaps even burns, before the outside of the food is hot. There are several explanations.

1. An item like a jam doughnut, where the centre has a high sugar content, will get hot before the sponge part, since microwaves are attracted to the sugar.
2. The same is true with high-fat foods, for microwaves are also attracted to fat. With eggs, for instance, the yolk, with its high fat content, will cook before the white is set.

Ceramic dishes

☐ Ceramic dishes may be used in the microwave, and are often marked as microwave-safe. Glass ceramic utensils can be used for microwaving and serving and can also be used for cooking on range tops and in conventional ovens.

Cereals

☐ Cereals such as porridge can be cooked in serving dishes or in quantity for the entire family. Cereals have a tendency to boil over, so use a large enough dish. Stir several times during cooking to distribute the heat evenly. During standing time you should leave cereals covered.

Cheese

☐ The moister or softer the cheese, the more quickly it will melt in the microwave. Moist and semi-aged cheeses melt very quickly, while the drier or aged cheeses, like Cheddar or Swiss, will soften but will not melt satisfactorily unless blended with some liquid. The processed cheeses available in slices, loaves and jars are high in moisture and are easy to use in the microwave.

☐ It is always best to use grated or finely chopped cheese in microwave recipes. It is easier to mix through the recipe and so cooks more evenly.

☐ Standing time is very important when cooking cheese. Undercook at first and test before cooking longer.

☐ Overcooked cheese becomes tough and stringy. To avoid this add cheese at the end of the cooking time, where appropriate to the recipe. Add a cheese topping during the last minute of the cooking time or during the standing time.

☐ Warm cold cheese in the microwave to make it easier to slice. Heat for 30–60 seconds on MEDIUM (50–60%).

☐ When softening cream cheese for pâtés and dips use MEDIUM-LOW (30–40%) if the cheese is straight from the refrigerator, so that it does not curdle.

☐ To quickly restore cheese to full flavour when it is cold from the refrigerator, heat on HIGH (100%) for about 10 seconds per 100 g.

☐ To cook cheese on toast, toast bread conventionally, then put cheese on top and cook on HIGH (100%) for 15 seconds or until cheese begins to bubble. But be careful not to overcook or the cheese will be tough.

☐ A quick cheese topping can be made by putting 250 g of processed cheese into a small jug and microwaving on MEDIUM (50–60%) for 3–4 minutes, or until the cheese has melted. Stir several times so that it is smooth, then pour over the dish. You can add 1 tablespoon of milk or even tomato juice, if you like, to make more of a sauce.

Cheesecake

☐ To remove cheesecake easily from a microwave dish, line the dish with several long strips of greaseproof paper, whose ends come up over the edge of the dish. Use the strips as handles to pull the cooked cheesecake from the dish.

☐ You can make a cheesecake base with shortbread biscuits and some good unsalted butter – this combination makes an excellent crust, too.

Chestnuts

☐ Slash crosswise through the skin at the flat end of chestnut shell. On a glass pie plate arrange 20–24 chestnuts in an even layer. Microwave on HIGH (100%) for 4–5 minutes, stirring every minute until the nuts are soft when squeezed. Stand for 5 minutes, then peel and eat warm. Chestnuts make a delicious treat in winter.

Chicken see also **Poultry**

☐ Always pierce the skin of chicken before cooking in the microwave to allow the steam to escape and thus prevent the skin popping.

☐ Chicken pieces will cook better if you marinate them overnight. Place on a rack and cook on MEDIUM (50–60%) for 10 minutes per 500 g. Stand for 5 minutes.

☐ Chicken fillets should be of even thickness for microwaving. Beat the thick end lightly to flatten.

☐ Always cover chicken pieces with a lid or paper towel to prevent them drying out during cooking.

☐ Chicken cooked in the microwave is excellent if you are dieting or cooking without fat. Be sure to remove the skin from chicken pieces first – this not only speeds up cooking but also prevents a fatty layer from forming on the surface of the meat.

☐ Roast whole chickens breast-side down first, so that the breast does not overcook and become too dry while the rest of the bird is still cooking.

☐ Chicken will not brown naturally in the microwave. To give it colour you can:
  - brown meat quickly in a frying pan on the stove
  - use a browning dish
  - brush the surface with melted butter and soy sauce, melted butter and paprika, a commercial browning agent, barbecue sauce or honey.

☐ Always stir chicken portions during cooking, moving those

on the outside to the middle of the dish and those at the centre to the edges, to ensure even cooking.

☐ A standing time of 10–15 minutes is essential for whole chickens. Portions need 5–10 minutes.

☐ Chicken is cooked once the juices run clear when the flesh is pierced with a sharp knife, or when an internal temperature of 82–85°C is reached.

Chicken livers

☐ Prick chicken livers with a fork before cooking so that the internal fat does not pop. Cover during cooking. Cook on MEDIUM (50%).

Children

☐ The microwave is an ideal way to let children help you with cooking: results are quick, and there is less danger of them burning themselves than with conventional cooking. If you use paper plates, there is less cleaning up to do.

☐ Popcorn (see page 81) is a great idea for children; melted cheese sandwiches are also easy.

☐ Try banana boats, too. Strip a section of skin back (but don't pull it right off), then cut the banana in half, lengthwise. Sprinkle with a few mini-marshmallows, chocolate chips or peanuts, replace the skin and microwave on HIGH (100%) for 1 minute.

China and ceramics

☐ China and pottery can be used in the microwave if they have no metal trim and are glazed. Unglazed earthenware or pottery can absorb microwaves and should not be used. Never use fine china in the microwave. Clay pots can be used as long as you presoak them according to manufacturer's instructions.

Chips

☐ Soggy chips or crackers, or other savoury snacks, can be crisped in the microwave: heat them on HIGH (100%) for 45–60 seconds, then stand for a few minutes.

Chocolate

☐ For the best results when using chocolate, use cooking chocolate with a copha base as it does not burn easily. Best quality chocolate will burn easily.

☐ To **melt** chocolate, break it into pieces and warm on MEDIUM (50–60%), stirring every minute: 100 g of chocolate will take about 2 minutes to melt. It will not actually melt in the usual sense; it retains its shape but will change from dull to glossy. When this happens, stir it through several times with a microwave-safe spoon.

☐ To reheat melted chocolate that has cooled and gone hard, warm on MEDIUM (50–60%) for 3 seconds and stir. Repeat at 5-second intervals until the desired consistency is reached. Adding milk or any other liquid to the chocolate can affect the cooking time, since liquids heat more rapidly.

☐ Chocolate chips are easy to melt.

☐ Do not cover chocolate when melting it in the microwave, as this will make it stiffen.

☐ When rolling chocolate for truffles or other sweets, work in a cool room to prevent the chocolate softening.

☐ Wrap chocolate tightly before refrigerating it, as it absorbs odours from other foods very easily.

Choko

☐ To cook choko, trim and cut as desired. Rinse and place in plastic freezer or oven bag. Secure. Cook on HIGH (100%): 2 whole chokos, sliced, will take about 6–8 minutes.

Christmas

☐ Using your microwave oven will make Christmas preparations much easier. One week in advance, make your microwave Christmas cake – it will cook in about 45 minutes.

☐ On the day, cook the plum pudding first. A traditional suet plum pudding will only take about 30 minutes to cook in the microwave, compared to the 6 hours or more of conventional steaming. It needs plenty of standing time, and while it is standing you can cook the turkey, followed by the vegetables, which need no standing time.

☐ After the turkey has been eaten you can reheat the plum pudding. Slices reheat best. Remember not to put any money or charms in a microwave pudding!

Chutney see **Jams, Jellies and Chutneys**

Citrus

☐ Citrus fruits will yield more juice if warmed in the microwave for 30–40 seconds on HIGH (100%) before squeezing.

Clarified butter see Butter

Cleaning see also Dirty dishes

☐ Microwave ovens are extremely easy to clean. There is no baked-on residue as in traditional dry heat cooking, so it's just a matter of getting a damp cloth and wiping your oven, preferably each time you use it. If you throw a damp cloth into the oven and microwave for 30–40 seconds, a bit of steam builds up, the cloth is hot and you can wipe the inner surfaces – simple as that.

☐ To remove smell from the oven after cooking fish in it, boil 4 cups water and 2 tablespoons lemon juice for 6–8 minutes on HIGH (100%).

Coconut

☐ To toast coconut, scatter 100 g on a microwave-safe plate and cook on HIGH (100%) for 4–6 minutes. Stir several times during cooking and check that it does not burn.

☐ To toast coconut for pie shells or bottoms of cakes, add 1 cup of flaked coconut to 3 tablespoons of melted, unsalted butter on a glass pie-plate. Microwave on HIGH (100%) for 4–6 minutes, stirring several times until coconut is brown.

☐ Mix coconut with breadcrumbs and dip fresh, white fish into the mixture, then gently fry in your browning plate – it's delicious.

Coffee

☐ If you make a whole pot of coffee you can store it in the fridge and reheat a cup at a time. Heating time is approximately 1 minute per cup on HIGH (100%).

☐ Heat water for a cup of instant coffee – let it settle for 30 seconds before adding the coffee otherwise you get a face full of hot water! A cup of water takes 2–2½ minutes to boil, depending on how cold the water was to start with.

☐ Irish coffee is popular any time of the year. Heat the liqueur for 10–20 seconds in your microwave and then pour into the drink. Don't bring to the boil or you will kill the alcohol. Reserve a small amount in a metal, long-handled spoon, light it and pour on top if you want something that looks rather dashing.

Cold spots

☐ Some areas inside the oven receive less microwave energy than others. The stirrer fan and turntable help eliminate this problem.

You can test for cold spots by placing several identical jugs or bowls of water around the oven: if they all boil at once, you have even microwave distribution. Most ovens have a greater concentration at the rim of the turntable than in the centre.

Colour see also **Browning, Toppings**

☐ Microwave cooking will not colour food the way a conventional oven does. This may not matter: a sponge to be used as the base of a flan needs to be as light as air, which is exactly what a microwave cake is, but its colour is irrelevant.

☐ **Meat** can be brushed with sauces to give colour (see **Browning**).

☐ **Fish, vegetables** and **fruit** do not require browning. Exceptions are roast vegetables, such as potatoes and parsnips, which are better cooked conventionally.

☐ A mixture of toasted breadcrumbs and grated cheese will give the top of a dish an even brown colour.

☐ **Cakes** can be coloured by using free-range eggs with very yellow yolks, wholemeal flour, brown sugar or spice. The colour of fruit cakes can be improved by adding coffee essence or Parisian essence to the mixture.

☐ **Savoury pastry** can be glazed before cooking with a mixture of soy sauce and water, or gravy browning.

☐ **Sweet pastry** can be glazed with brown sugar dissolved in water.

☐ Wholemeal flour will also improve the colour and texture of pastry.

☐ **Biscuits** will brown in the microwave because of their high sugar content.

☐ Crumble toppings on fruit puddings cook well, but make

them with wholemeal flour and brown sugar to ensure a good colour.

Combination ovens

☐ A combination oven cooks both by microwaves and by conventional convection heating. Some may also have a conventional grill.

☐ The microwave energy and convection heat can work together to produce traditional crisp results in a much quicker cooking time than conventional methods. They can also work independently of each other.

☐ Traditional roast meat and vegetables can be cooked well in a combination oven, more successfully than in a microwave alone.

☐ As with ordinary microwave ovens, you can't use metal utensils in a combination oven. Ovenproof glassware and ceramic dishes are ideal for combination ovens.

Composition of food

☐ The kind of food you are cooking will make a difference to the cooking time. Microwaves are attracted to fat and sugar, so foods high in these ingredients will cook faster than foods high in liquid. It takes longer to cook the same weight of food with a high liquid content, e.g. meat or vegetables, than something with little liquid, such as a cake, bread or biscuits.

Conduction

☐ Conduction is when heat is transferred from something hot

to an adjoining cold spot. Microwaves heat the outside 4 cm of food, but the inside must cook by the outside heat being transferred to it by conduction. This is why some foods need standing time after cooking, to allow the heat to reach the centre.

Containers see **Dishes, Plastic, Utensils**

Convection ovens

☐ These are conventional ovens with a fan. The hot air, circulated by the oven fan, heats food faster than non-moving air would.

Convenience foods

☐ Microwave ovens are perfect for convenience foods, as it is so quick to reheat from frozen. Many packs of frozen food now carry microwave instructions.

☐ Foods containing pastry or bread won't have an oven-crisp texture if heated in the microwave.

☐ Frozen pies need a combination of microwave and convection to achieve a crispy crust.

☐ Try warming pies in your microwave then crisping in a conventional oven.

Converting conventional recipes

☐ Use a microwave power corresponding to the level of conventional heat required: instead of a very hot oven, use HIGH (100%); instead of a moderate oven, use MEDIUM (50–60%);

and instead of a low oven, use MEDIUM-LOW (30–40%).

☐ Cut the cooking time to a quarter of the conventional time, and then check. Usually a converted recipe takes about one-third of the time of conventional cooking, but it is wise to check after one-quarter, and to cook for a few more minutes if necessary.

☐ Remember to allow standing time at the end of microwaving.

☐ Reduce the liquid in the recipe by one-third (except for cakes, see below).

☐ Start by converting a familiar recipe, then you will know what it should look and taste like when it is cooked.

☐ Reduce the quantities of herbs, spices, seasonings and wine in converted recipes as their flavours remain strong after microwaving and may overpower.

☐ Use very little water when adapting vegetable recipes as they are naturally moist.

☐ You may have to precook some vegetables for casseroles as vegetables cook more slowly than meat in a microwave.

☐ Cakes need *more* liquid when cooked in a microwave as they tend to dry out. They also need less raising agents. So reduce baking powder, etc., by a quarter and increase the liquid by a quarter. You will not need to beat the mixture as much as you would normally.

☐ Biscuits need to have their flour increased by about a fifth and the mixture will be very stiff. If the dough is chilled for 30 minutes before cooking the biscuits will be crisper.

☐ Use brown sugar and wholemeal flour in pudding, cake and biscuit recipes where a brown colour is desired.

☐ **Don't** try to convert recipes for roast potatoes, Yorkshire pudding, soufflés, pizzas or pies. Pastry is difficult and won't brown. Pavlovas are not successful – in the microwave they cook more like a meringue.

☐ **Never** deep fry in a microwave. This is extremely dangerous.

Cooking bags see also **Plastic**

☐ Cooking bags are most useful for cooking roasts, whole chickens or less tender cuts of meat that need moisture for tenderising (e.g. silverside). Be sure to discard the metal twist tie and cut a strip off the bag from the open end to use as a tie, or use a rubber band or piece of string. Puncture several holes in the bag near the opening.

Cooking rack

☐ Another name for a roasting rack.

Cooking times

☐ Because food cooks so fast in a microwave always follow the recommended cooking time in a recipe.

☐ Cooking times will also depend on your particular oven, as the power output of different models at present in the shops ranges from 600 to 1000 watts, so make sure you know what your oven's output is. Smaller output ovens will take about 10% longer to cook a dish. Most recipes are given for 650–700 watts, so if you have an older, 400–500-watt oven you will

have to increase the timing. Conversely, if you have a powerful, 1000-watt oven, you will have to reduce the power used
or the timing.

☐ Timing will depend on the amount and the temperature of
the food you are cooking. Food from the refrigerator will take
longer than food at room temperature.

☐ If you double the recipe quantity, you will need to multiply
the cooking time by 1½. If you halve the quantity, decrease
time by a third.

☐ Always aim to undercook. You can put the food back in the
oven if necessary, but it is all too easy to overcook in the
microwave, and ruin your food.

☐ Food containing a lot of water and sugar, such as fruit, cooks
very quickly.

Corn on the cob see Sweetcorn

Corned beef

☐ Corned beef can be cooked in a bag to save on washing up.
The bag will also help to retain moisture.

Cornflour

☐ Use cornflour for thickening casseroles, sauces, etc., instead
of flour; cornflour contains less gluten and if used, the results
are often less gluey than with plain flour.

Cost

☐ Microwave ovens do not use a lot of electricity and so are cheap to run. Even if cooking time seems long, for instance for stews, rice or pasta, it will still be much cheaper to cook these dishes in the microwave than conventionally.

Covering dishes see also **Paper, Plastic, Serviettes**

☐ In general, food you would cover when cooking conventionally should be covered in the microwave.

☐ Covering food shortens the cooking time and keeps the moisture in.

☐ Covered food needs only a small amount of liquid.

☐ Don't cover anything that needs to be crisp: cakes, bread, pastry and pies.

☐ Plastic wrap is a very useful cover. If a lot of steam will be created during cooking make sure that the wrap is vented in some way, either by piercing it or by not completely sealing the wrap.

☐ Never cover a browning dish.

☐ Kitchen paper towels can be used as loose covers when reheating bread or pastry: they will absorb moisture. They are also very useful to cook bacon, chicken and fish.

☐ Microwave-safe plates make excellent covers for dishes.

☐ Waxed greaseproof paper is ideal to cover food that does not need trapped steam for tenderising. It forms a loose seal similar to partial covering in conventional cooking. Use to prevent spattering when heating milk, or as a tent with poultry or seafood.

☐ Roasting or freezer bags can be used to enclose a dish completely. Ensure they are microwave-safe before using. They should be pierced to allow steam to escape.

Crackers
☐ Soggy crackers can be crisped by reheating for a few seconds.

Crackling
☐ To crisp pork crackling, carve serving-sized pieces and place between paper towels. Microwave on HIGH (100%) for 2 minutes at a time until the crackling hardens to the desired crunchiness.

Cream
☐ If cream has come straight from the refrigerator, you can warm it for a few seconds on DEFROST (30%) before using it in a recipe, to speed cooking.
☐ Never boil a sauce to which you have added cream, or it will curdle. Cook the sauce gently on MEDIUM (50–60%).

Cream cheese see Cheese

Creaming
☐ Creaming butter and sugar together will be much easier if you soften the butter on MEDIUM-LOW/DEFROST (30–40%) first. Don't let it melt, though.

Croutons
☐ Croutons can be made very quickly in a microwave oven. Cut 2 thick slices of bread into cubes. Heat 45 g of butter on

HIGH (100%) for 1 minute, then toss the cubes of bread into the butter and cook on HIGH for another minute. Drain the croutons on kitchen paper and serve with soup.

Cupcakes see **Patty cakes**

Curdling
☐ Recipes whose ingredients include mayonnaise, sour cream, cheese, yoghurt or cream should always be heated gently on MEDIUM (50–60%) to prevent curdling.

Currants see **Dried fruit**

Custard see also **Baked custard**
☐ Prevent custard boiling over by using a container twice the capacity of the ingredients.
☐ Custards will cook and set best if all the ingredients are at room temperature. Heat milk and cream on DEFROST (30%) for 30 seconds before using.

D

Defrost setting
☐ DEFROST is 30% power.
☐ Many ovens have a special DEFROST button.
☐ DEFROST is an excellent power for slow cooking stocks and stews. It can be used towards the end of cooking to tenderise slightly chewy meats.

Defrosting

☐ Always elevate food to be defrosted. This prevents the food sitting in moisture, and allows a quicker and more even defrost.

☐ Microwaves are attracted to liquid, so if the food you are defrosting produces a lot of water, pour it off, or mop it up with paper towels. Defrosting will be quicker if you do. This particularly applies to meat and poultry.

☐ Always allow standing time at the end of the DEFROST cycle. Don't continue defrosting for a long time without a break as the food may start to cook.

☐ Turn a large piece of **meat** over three to four times during defrosting.

☐ Separate pieces of **fish** as they start to thaw, or else the outside ones will begin to cook.

☐ All **fish and shellfish** should be completely cold when thawed. Remove from the oven when still slightly icy and let defrosting complete during standing time.

☐ **Poultry** must always be completely thawed before cooking to prevent bacteria growing in the meat.

☐ If part of the food starts to thaw faster than the rest, you can shield it by putting foil over it, attached with wooden toothpicks (make sure the foil isn't touching the sides of the oven).

☐ Home-frozen food takes longer to thaw than commercially frozen food, because it contains larger ice-crystals.

☐ If you only want to defrost some of a block of minced meat, say, you can shield one end and return it to the freezer when the unshielded, defrosted end is soft enough to be cut.

☐ Stand **bread**, **pastry** and **cakes** on paper towels when defrosting to prevent sogginess.

☐ Never let **bread** overheat: it will become stale and hard very easily.

☐ Be very careful when defrosting uncooked **pastry**. If it becomes warm take it out of the oven immediately. If uncooked pastry warms the fat in it melts, the pastry will crack when it is rolled and the finished, cooked pastry will be tough and dry.

☐ Because **fruit** is high in sugar, and microwaves are attracted to sugar, be careful when defrosting fruit or it will begin to cook, losing its shape and juice. After defrosting, fruit should still be firm and cold.

☐ Never cover **fruit** when defrosting, as the air must circulate around it.

Delay

☐ A programme available on some microwave ovens. It allows the microwave to be set on a cooking cycle later on, and may also be used as standing time between cooking on two different power settings, i.e. between defrosting and cooking a casserole from the freezer.

Dieting

☐ Microwaving is an ideal cooking method for dieters as you

don't need to use fat or oil at all. Poaching and steaming are easy in the microwave, and retain the essential nutrients in your food.

Dips

☐ Dips and hors d'oeuvres that contain mayonnaise, sour cream, natural cheese, yoghurt or cream should be heated gently on MEDIUM (50–60%) or MEDIUM-LOW/DEFROST (30–40%) to avoid curdling.

Dirty dishes

☐ Microwaving allows you to cook and serve in the same dish and thus reduces washing up.

☐ Scorched dishes are easy to clean in the microwave: fill the dish with water, add 2 tablespoons of baking soda and microwave on HIGH (100%) for 5–6 minutes. This is also a good way of cleaning a browning plate.

Dish lids

☐ Lids may be put upside down on dishes to cook two recipes at once. Lids may also be used for cooking flans and vegetables.

Dishes see also **Equipment, Heat retention, Utensils**

☐ Food will cook more evenly in round dishes than in square ones. Curved corners help stop food overcooking at the edges.

☐ Shallow dishes are better than deep ones as microwaves

work more efficiently when the food to be cooked is spread thinly over a large surface.

☐ Liquids are best heated in tall, narrow containers, such as jugs.

☐ Make sure that dishes are large enough to allow stirring.

☐ Remember that milk can double in volume when it boils, so use a large enough dish.

☐ When buying large dishes for the microwave take along a paper template of the turntable. If the dish is larger than the template it will hit the oven's sides.

Dog food

☐ Don't forget you can defrost the dog's meat in the microwave oven before you chop it up.

DON'Ts

☐ Don't ever try to deep-fry in the microwave. It is extremely dangerous.

☐ Don't operate the oven if it is empty. It will be damaged.

☐ Don't put metal or dishes with metal trim in the microwave.

☐ Don't add salt when microwaving, it makes the food dry and tough. Add it when cooking is over.

☐ Don't use newspaper, recycled paper or brown paper in the microwave: tiny impurities in the paper can cause arcing.

☐ Don't dry wet fabric or paper in the microwave. They could catch fire.

Doneness

☐ A term used to describe the desired degree of cooking. Remember that it isn't possible to judge doneness by the degree of browning.

Dried fruit

☐ To plump up dried fruit, add 1–3 tablespoons of water, wine or fruit juice for each 150 g of fruit (the amount of liquid will depend on the size of the fruit), cover and heat on HIGH (100%) for 1–2 minutes. Stir well and allow to cool.

Drinks see also **Coffee, Tea, Toppings**

☐ Drinks can be heated in the microwave in heavy glasses (*not* lead crystal), glazed pottery cups, paper cups and plastic foam cups.

Drying see also **Pot pourri**

☐ **Flowers** can be dried on a small scale, a few at a time.
☐ Choose flowers that are firm, cool, dry and sturdy, preferably not in full bloom. If the blooms are full blown they tend to lose their petals when dried. The most successful flowers for drying are carnations, daisies and daffodils. Stay away from magnolias and dahlias, which do not dry well.
☐ Flowers that are yellow retain their colour. White tends to become a bit grey. Bright red and blue flowers turn purple.
☐ Put a couple of inches of cat litter into a container, place flowers evenly in the litter. Then sift more litter over until the flowers are covered. Place a cup of water in the back of your

oven so that the microwave has something to work on and then put the dish with the flowers towards the centre of the turntable. Heat on HIGH (100%) for ½–3½ minutes (the time will vary with the number of flowers). Let the flowers stand in the container for 30 minutes, continuing to dry. Gently remove your flowers with some of the litter and store.

☐ **Herbs**: put a paper towel on the turntable, spread the leaves of the herb over it, and put another paper towel on top. Put a cup of water in the oven (herbs contain so little moisture you can damage the oven if you don't). Then either microwave on HIGH (100%) for 30 seconds at a time, until the herbs are just slightly moist (they will dry completely on cooling). This takes about 2–4 minutes. You can also microwave on DEFROST (30%) for 3–4 minutes.

☐ The actual time taken to dry will depend on the herb: thin, flat-leaved herbs will dry fastest. Parsley will dry faster than rosemary, for example.

☐ Be careful not to over-dry – herbs can burn.

☐ **Rind**: place grated orange or lemon rind on a paper towel, spread out evenly, and microwave on DEFROST (30%) for 30 minutes, rearranging frequently. The rind should be very hard after cooking, and can be stored in an airtight container.

☐ **Fruit** can be dried in the microwave, but those with a high sugar content may burn (apricots are tricky to dry). Slice the fruit and arrange in a layer on kitchen paper. Microwave on LOW (30–40%) or DEFROST (30%). Pineapple takes 18–22 minutes; one green apple 10–12 minutes; one peach 10–12 minutes.

Duck see also **Poultry**

☐ Pierce the duck before cooking to allow the fat to run out.

☐ Always cook duck on a roasting rack breast-side down so that it does not sit in fat that has run out.

☐ Because of its layer of fat, duck *will* brown in the microwave.

☐ Start cooking the duck breast-side down and turn over half-way through.

☐ Do not overcook duck or it will become very dry.

E

Egg

☐ Eggs are hard to cook in a microwave: they are delicate and easily overcooked, and microwaves are attracted more by the fat-rich yolk than the white, so the yolk has a tendency to cook faster.

☐ Always use eggs at room temperature for best results.

☐ **Scrambled eggs** are easiest, because the yolk and white are mixed. Use water instead of milk for extra fluffiness. Use a large container as scrambled eggs expand rapidly. If you want to add grated cheese, do this after cooking and it will melt in.

☐ **Poached eggs**: prick the yolk before cooking, otherwise the egg will explode; use a custard cup – an egg will not cook in a saucer – and cover the container for best results. Always cook on MEDIUM-LOW (30%). Stop cooking when white is nearly set as standing time will complete cooking.

☐ **Fried eggs**: prick the yolk before cooking on a browning plate.

☐ **Boiled eggs**: prick the blunt end before cooking. Wrap each egg in foil. Place in a bowl and cover with luke-warm water. Microwave on HIGH (100%) for 6–10 minutes for soft-boiled. If you want a hard-boiled egg for mashing cook in a custard cup, as for poached egg, until yolk is firm.

☐ **Omelettes** are best cooked covered. When cooked they will be set on the outside but the centre will still be moist, so allow to stand 3–5 minutes. If you cook until the centre is dry the omelette will be tough.

☐ It is easy to reheat left-over egg dishes in the microwave, but use MEDIUM-LOW (30–40%) to avoid toughening.

☐ Sauces containing eggs should be cooked on MEDIUM-LOW (30–40%).

Eggplant

☐ To cook, slice as desired, rinse and place in a plastic freezer or oven bag. Secure. Cook on HIGH (100%): 250 g will take 4–6 minutes.

Empty

☐ Never operate your oven when it is empty or you may damage it.

Entertaining see also **Appetisers, Canapés**

☐ The secret of successful entertaining is to do as much as you can in advance, as the big strength of a microwave oven is its reheating capacity.

☐ Always slightly undercook in the first instance so that when you reheat the food will be exactly right, not dry or over-cooked.

☐ Always cover food when reheating it, or it will dry out.

☐ If you are cooking just before eating, plan your menu. If dessert is to be a hot pudding, cook it first, as it will need the most standing time, then cook the meat and finally your vegetables.

Equipment see also **Dishes, Utensils,** individual entries for dishes

☐ Useful items of cookware include a roasting rack, a cake ring or loop, a browning dish, a muffin pan, platestackers, and casserole dishes – usually in three sizes.

F

Face pack

☐ For normal skin, try this sage and apple face pack. Core an apple and cook on HIGH (100%) for 2–3 minutes. You should then be able to slip the skin off the apple, which will be a pulp. Add 2 tablespoons of honey and 2 dessertspoons of chopped fresh sage. Mix well, and leave to cool. When cool pat over skin and leave for 15 minutes. Rinse off with warm water and then splash your face with cold water.

Fat

☐ Microwaving is a moist cooking form so you need the barest minimum of cooking fat. Remember to cut it right down in any recipe you are converting.

Fibres

☐ To help you judge timing in your microwave, imagine all solid food is made up of fibres. Tight-fibred foods, such as meat, potatoes or carrots, will cook slower than loose-fibred, light food such as bread.

Figs

☐ Figs are very healthy: they contribute calcium, potassium, magnesium and Vitamin B6 to your diet and their sodium content is very low. So why not incorporate them in breads, muffins and desserts? But be careful: they are high in natural sugar, so reduce other sugars in your recipe; and because sugar attracts microwaves be sure to chop the figs finely and stir well to distribute them through the mixture, or it will cook unevenly.

☐ For a perfect snack, heat figs in the microwave – delicious!

Fire

- [ ] If a fire starts in your oven, press Stop and turn off power at wall switch. DO NOT OPEN DOOR.

Fish see also **Shellfish**

- [ ] When cooking fish make sure that you dry the fish thoroughly. If you are baking it, raise it on a roasting rack or line the dish with paper towels so that excess moisture is drained away during the cooking.
- [ ] Overlap the tail ends of any thin fillets for even cooking, with the thicker ends towards the outside of the dish.
- [ ] To enhance its colour you can sprinkle a little paprika on fish, or brush it with soy sauce.
- [ ] Prick the eye of a fish before cooking so that it does not leap out of the socket during cooking. You may also need to cover the tails of whole fish with a little foil during the first half of cooking to prevent them overcooking.
- [ ] Before frying any white fish, dip them into a mixture of toasted breadcrumbs and coconut to make a delicious coating. Fry the fish in your browning plate.
- [ ] To steam fish, don't add water. Just cover the fish with a moistened paper towel.
- [ ] Frozen fish that has been defrosted will take a little longer to cook than fresh fish – about ½–1 minute per 500 g of fish.
- [ ] Fish cooks very, very quickly, so be careful. Take it out of the oven when it is just opaque, as it will continue to cook while it stands.

☐ If you are cooking fish with other ingredients, such as vegetables, soften the vegetables first as the fish will cook very fast once it is added.

☐ When cooking whole fish, lightly score the skin to allow steam to escape.

☐ Commercially packaged battered fish does not cook well in the microwave: the results are soggy, not crisp.

☐ Fish tends to dry out while cooking, so always cover the dish with a lid or paper towel. If the fish doesn't have a sauce, dot it with butter or brush it with oil before cooking.

☐ Fish doesn't reheat well, so it is always best to cook it at the last minute. If you must reheat, do so on MEDIUM-LOW (30–40%), to prevent the fish becoming dry.

Flambéing see also **Brandy**

☐ Warm 2 tablespoons of spirit in a small bowl or jug for 30–40 seconds on HIGH (100%). Ignite with a taper and pour over dish.

Flowers, drying see **Drying**

Foil see **Aluminium foil**

Freezing see also **Blanching**

☐ The microwave is an invaluable adjunct to your freezer. Food can be defrosted quicker, with less liquid loss.

☐ Freeze extra food in one-person serves for convenient reheating.

☐ To defrost soups and casseroles: 4 cups will take about 10 minutes on DEFROST (30%); 8 cups will take 16 minutes. Then let stand and reheat on MEDIUM (50–60%): 4 cups will take 10–12 minutes; 8 cups 16–18 minutes. Stir during reheating for best results.

☐ Cottage pie freezes and reheats well. Defrost a 1-litre container for 10 minutes; a 2-litre container will take 15–20 minutes.

☐ Blanch small quantities of vegetables in the microwave before freezing.

French toast

☐ This can be made on the browning plate. Cook 2 slices on HIGH (100%) for 1½ minutes.

Fruit see also Drying

☐ Stewed fruit is best cooked in a heatproof container. Be careful not to add too much water: 1–2 tablespoons should be sufficient, but the exact amount will depend on how juicy the fruit is. Cook covered for about 6–8 minutes per 500 g of fruit, stirring two or three times during cooking.

Fruit juices

☐ Take chill off your juices by warming them for 15–20 seconds in the microwave.

☐ Remember Vitamin C is destroyed by heat, so if you are using the microwave to defrost frozen orange juice only partially thaw it out.

G

Garlic
- [ ] Cloves of garlic can be peeled easily by placing the cloves on a rack and heating for 30 seconds per clove on HIGH (100%). The garlic will then slide out of the skin.
- [ ] Dishes containing garlic should only be frozen for weeks rather than months as the garlic can give the dish a slightly musty flavour over a long period.
- [ ] Garlic bread only takes 1 minute on HIGH (100%). Wrap the prepared French stick in kitchen paper; turn over half-way through heating.
- [ ] Garlic powder is perfectly safe to use in the microwave, as is fresh garlic, of course. Garlic salt is not, see below.

Garlic salt
- [ ] Garlic salt contains salt and therefore should not be sprinkled on food before cooking in a microwave, as the food will become tough and dry.

Gelatine
- [ ] Gelatine can be easily dissolved in the microwave. Mix with water and cook on HIGH (100%) for 20–30 seconds. Allow to stand until liquid becomes clear (up to 1 minute).

Glass
- [ ] Do not use glass jars or bottles in the microwave oven

unless they are designed for cooking, as jars can break as the food gets hot. Don't heat glass for more than 1 minute. Ensure metal lids and trims are off before microwaving.

☐ Cooking in a glass container will take a little longer than in microwave-safe plastic containers.

☐ Special ovenware glass, such as Pyrex, is fine for the microwave. If you use clear glass for pies, bread and cakes you can watch for 'doneness' through the base.

☐ Never put fine crystal glass into the microwave – it usually contains lead, and may crack when heated.

Glazing

☐ Most glazes have a high sugar content, and can burn quickly. When you are glazing meat, it should be almost cooked through or, in the case of a fully cooked ham, heated through, before glazing. Glaze should be added during the last quarter of cooking time. Give the meat an extra brushing of sauce just before the standing time.

Glue

☐ To dry glue quickly, put freshly glued items in the oven and microwave on HIGH (100%) for a minute or two. Don't leave them in too long: paper and wood can burn if they are over-heated.

Ground beef see Minced beef

H

Hamburgers see also **Burgers**

☐ One hamburger can be cooked on a paper plate. For more, use the muffin or patty cake dish to make neat, individual hamburgers. Jazz up these baby hamburgers by adding grated cheese, sour cream, mushrooms, bacon, green pepper or onion. If you are adding onion, green pepper or grated carrot, first soften the vegetables in your microwave oven as suggested for casseroles.

☐ One burger takes about 1½–2 minutes to cook, on MEDIUM-HIGH (70%).

☐ If you barbecue or grill hamburgers, cook extra and freeze them. When reheated in the microwave, they will have a delicious grilled flavour.

Handicapped microwavers

☐ Microwave cooking is ideal for handicapped people. The oven can be situated at any convenient height, and the front touch controls are easy for the physically handicapped to use. It is simpler for a blind person than a conventional oven; and for older, housebound people it gives independence to reheat meals when they can no longer cook for themselves. Because the oven does not get hot it cannot burn the user, and the plastic cookware is light, unbreakable and easy to clean.

Heat retention

☐ Although many dishes remain cool during cooking in the microwave the food in them will become very hot, and where the food touches it, the dish may also become hot. So be careful when taking dishes out of the oven. Browning dishes become very hot and can burn.

Herb tea

☐ Many herbs can be made into teas. Why not try rosemary tea before bedtime if you are feeling twitchy? Dry a sprig of rosemary in the microwave (see **Drying**), put the sprig in a mug, cover with water and bring to the boil for 2–2½ minutes. Remove the rosemary, keep the mug covered for a couple of minutes and then drink.

Herbs see also **Drying, Spices**

☐ Because microwave cooking takes less time than conventional cooking, flavours aren't absorbed as much and are stronger. Use less herbs than you would normally.

☐ If you are cutting down on salt in your cooking, add herbs instead to highlight the flavour of the food.

☐ ¼ teaspoon of dried herbs equals 1 teaspoon of fresh.

High setting only

☐ If your microwave has only one setting, i.e. HIGH (100%), and you want to cook on MEDIUM (50–60%), try putting a cup or two of water in a glass jug in a corner of your oven along with the food you are cooking. The water will absorb some of the microwaves and slow down the cooking.

Hollandaise sauce

☐ Always cook Hollandaise sauce on DEFROST (30%) and stir frequently.

Honey

☐ To clarify honey that has become sugary, microwave on HIGH (100%) for 1–2 minutes. Be sure to remove the metal lid before heating.

Hot towels see Towels

I

━━∿∿∿∿━━

Ice-cream

☐ Soften frozen ice-cream for 30–60 seconds on MEDIUM-LOW/DEFROST (30%) to make it easy to scoop and serve.

Ice-cream containers

☐ Ice-cream containers were made for freezing food and are not suitable for using in the microwave, as the food can absorb small quantities of toxic substances from the container.

J

~~~~~

Jams, jellies and chutneys

☐ Jams, jellies and chutneys are great made in the microwave as they retain their fresh flavour and colour. However, fruit juices do not evaporate, so you may need to use pectin or Jamsetta to get your jam to set.

☐ You can make an easy 15-minute jam from any fruit. You need: 1 kg washed fruit, placed in a deep bowl. Cover and cook in the microwave for 5 minutes on HIGH (100%). Add 1 kg of sugar and cook for another 5 minutes. Add ½ packet Jamsetta with strawberries, ⅛ packet for any other fruit, then cook on HIGH (100%) a further 5 minutes. Cool and bottle.

☐ Always use a heatproof large bowl when making jam or preserves. Fruit contains a lot of sugar and jams can boil over rapidly. Don't try to cook more than 1.5 kg of fruit at one time as you would need a dish larger than the oven! If the mixture looks like boiling over, give it a stir to distribute the heat evenly.

☐ Put a paper towel under the jam container so that if it does boil over cleaning up is easy.

☐ To test if jam will set, dip a large metal spoon into the jam. If the syrup coats the back of the spoon, the jam will set. Or put a drop on a chilled saucer and see if the skin wrinkles when it is cool.

☐ For a special gift, place a bunch of grapes in the jars before adding the jam. This jam will have to be eaten within two weeks.

☐ You can sterilise jam jars in the microwave. Put 2–3 cm boiled water in the clean jars. Cook, uncovered, on HIGH (100%), until the water boils. Remove from oven, put tops on, and leave while making jam. Empty water out when you are ready to fill jars.

☐ Use your microwave to melt jam for glazing fruit flans.

Jars

☐ Don't use glass jars for cooking food in the microwave unless they are for cooking purposes. Jars can break as the food gets hot.

Kebabs

☐ Don't use metal skewers for kebabs. Use wooden ones instead.

☐ Put the meat and vegetables on different skewers as the meat may need a little longer time than the vegetables. Cook the vegetables while the meat kebabs are standing.

☐ Cook the kebabs on a microwave-safe rack, or hung over a shallow baking dish. If you prefer your kebabs seared, use a browning plate.

Kidney
- [ ] Pierce the skin of kidney before cooking. Cook on MEDIUM (50%):
  125 g will take 2–4 minutes, with 3 minutes' standing time;
  250 g will take 3–5 minutes, with 3 minutes' standing time;
  500 g will take 6–8 minutes, with 5 minutes' standing time.

Kids see Children

Kohlrabi
- [ ] Trim and cut as desired. Rinse and place in plastic freezer or oven bag. Secure. Cook on HIGH (100%): 250 g will take 8–10 minutes.

L

Lamb see also Meat, Roasting
- [ ] Cook roast lamb on a microwave rack above a baking dish, to allow the fat to drain from the meat. Tent with a paper towel or baking parchment to prevent spattering.
- [ ] If cooking rack of lamb or chops, place the bone ends towards the oven's centre.
- [ ] Cook leg or shoulder of lamb on MEDIUM-HIGH (70%) for 8–10 minutes per 500 g if you like your meat medium; 12–14 minutes per 500 g for well done. Let stand 15–20 minutes.
- [ ] Cook lamb chops on HIGH (100%):

2 chops will take 5–7 minutes, with 3 minutes' standing time;
4 chops will take 8–10 minutes, with 4 minutes' standing time;
500 g will take 10–12 minutes, with 5 minutes' standing time.
- ☐ Lamb shanks need slower cooking on MEDIUM (50–60%).
- ☐ Leftover lamb can be made into a casserole with some tangy tomato or chilli sauce, or into a spicy curry. For an easy lunch dish, slice the lamb thinly, spread with coarsely-ground mustard, top with a slice of mild, white cheese such as mozzarella or provolone and arrange between slices of rye bread. Cook on MEDIUM-HIGH (70%) until the cheese melts – about a minute or so.

Leeks
- ☐ Wash and slice. Put into plastic oven or freezer bag and secure. Cook on HIGH (100%): 250 g will take 4–6 minutes.

Lemons
- ☐ To get more juice from a lemon, heat for 30–40 seconds on HIGH (100%), stand, then squeeze the juice.

Lids
- ☐ If a plastic lid is stuck on a bottle or jar, microwave on HIGH (100%) for 10 seconds to loosen.

Liquids
- ☐ Microwaves cook by working on water molecules in the food and the moisture content of recipes has to be adjusted to suit this. Cakes need to be wetter than conventional recipes,

but vegetables, which contain a lot of water, need very little added.

☐ Remember that liquids don't evaporate in a microwave, as there is no direct heat. So reduce the liquid in recipes by at least one-quarter (except for cakes). When making gravy for casseroles and puddings, you may need to add a little more thickening agent than usual as there is no means of reducing the fluids. A good thickening agent is cornflour which contains less gluten than other flours.

Liver
☐ Pierce the skin and cook with 1 tablespoon of oil or butter. Cook on MEDIUM (50%) for 5–7 minutes per 250 g, with 3 minutes' standing time.

M

Marinades
☐ Marinades add flavour to meat, and also help to brown and tenderise it. Marinating overnight is best.
☐ Don't use a marinade high in salt, as this will make the meat tougher instead of tenderer when it is cooked!

Marmalade see **Jams, Jellies and Chutneys**

Marshmallows

☐ A fun trick with marshmallows is to place a few in the microwave and cook for 2 or 3 minutes on HIGH (100%). They will grow huge, four times their normal size. They are overcooked and inedible, but children love to watch them grow.

Marzipan

☐ Soften hard marzipan by heating on DEFROST (30%) for 1½–2 minutes. It will then be easy to roll out.

Meat see also **Beef, Kidney, Lamb, Liver, Pork, Veal**

☐ Choose joints as evenly shaped as possible. If there are thinner parts they will cook faster than the thicker, so will need shielding with foil (the ends of lamb legs, the tips of bolar beef).

☐ Don't try to cook a joint heavier than about 2 kg in the microwave.

☐ Trim fat to give an even cover. If the joint doesn't have much fat, e.g. veal, you can secure bacon strips to the meat with wooden toothpicks. A joint with little or no fat tends to toughen and has to be cooked very carefully on MEDIUM (50–60%).

☐ Brown roasts in a browning dish at the start of cooking. If you don't have a browning dish, brown the joint on top of the stove first.

☐ Cook a joint on a roasting rack, to ensure it is not steaming or stewing in its own juice. Cover it with paper towel to absorb excess moisture.

☐ Use a microwave meat thermometer for best results with roasts. Always cook to a lower temperature than you would conventionally as temperatures rise on standing. For small roasts 5°C lower is sufficient; for medium 10°C; for large 15°C.

☐ Always place the thickest part of the meat on the edge of the turntable where the microwaves can reach it.

☐ Don't wrap meat in foil when standing as the steam will give the meat a boiled flavour. Tent with foil instead, shiny side down.

☐ When cooking a pot roast make sure the dish has a tight lid.

☐ Long slow simmering helps tenderise tougher meats. You can cook meat on DEFROST (30%) with good results.

☐ Don't salt meat before cooking as this will cause toughening.

☐ Only tender cuts are really suitable for roasting in the microwave. For beef this means fillet, sirloin or rib; for veal it means fillet, loin, rump or leg; for lamb the choice is leg, loin or chump; and for pork fillet, loin and leg.

☐ Less tender cuts can be marinated and pot-roasted, or casseroled. These include beef topside, skirt, blade and silverside; lamb shoulder, breast and shank; veal shoulder, neck and breast; and pork shoulder, neck, spare ribs and hand. They should be cooked on MEDIUM (50–60%) or MEDIUM-LOW/DEFROST (30–40%).

Meatloaf

☐ Meatloaf is best cooked in a ring container. Timing is about 10–12 minutes per 500 g on MEDIUM-HIGH (70%).

☐ Meatloaf won't brown in the microwave. To help its appearance you can add 1 teaspoon of Parisian essence to the ingredients, or browning sauce; you can also top the meatloaf with breadcrumbs, which will brown, or a tomato sauce, or cheese at the end of cooking.

Medium power

☐ 50–60% of HIGH, used for poaching and baking.

Medium-high power

☐ 70–80% of HIGH, used for roasting and reheating.

Menu planning

☐ This takes a little bit of practice. You will need to microwave food that needs the longest cooking and standing time first, usually roasts, casseroles or large pieces of poultry. They can either be cooked earlier in the day or the day before and reheated as needed. Things that need shorter cooking and standing times, such as vegetables, fish and fruit desserts, are microwaved closer to serving time. At the last moment microwave the small items such as bread rolls and quick reheats.

☐ Many desserts can be pre-cooked and reheated, so they can be prepared early in the day.

☐ Partially microwave one item while you prepare another. You can take out the first item from the oven while you cook another dish, then return the first dish to the oven to complete its cooking time.

Meringue

☐ Meringues are delicious cooked in the microwave, but the basic recipe differs from the conventional one, so don't try to convert.

☐ To make meringue, whisk one egg white until frothy, then add 300–350 g icing sugar (the exact amount depends on the size of the egg). Work the sugar in until the mixture is stiff, and then knead by hand for 2–3 minutes until mixture forms a smooth ball. Cut off small amounts and form into balls – this amount will make 48 meringues. Cook on greaseproof paper on HIGH (100%): 6 meringues will take 1½ minutes.

Metal

☐ **Don't** put any metal in the microwave.

☐ Watch out for hidden metal wires inside twists for sealing bags. If you are going to tie up an oven bag, we suggest you cut a ribbon from the bag or use a rubber band or string.

☐ Some cups have metal reinforcements in their handles, which will cause arcing.

Microcrisp

☐ This wrap enables you to cook crisp pastry, pies and pizzas in the microwave. Wrap the food in the Microcrisp, with the white side against the food, but do not seal the ends. The food must then be put on a special 'dual ovenable' rack (these can be used in conventional ovens as well as in the microwave). An ordinary rack *cannot* be used as it will distort. Follow the directions on the Microcrisp pack for power and timings.

Microwaves

☐ Microwaves are high frequency, short-wave, electro-magnetic waves, like television and radio waves. They penetrate about 4 cm into food, and are particularly attracted to liquids, fats and sugars. The microwaves make molecules in the food vibrate extremely fast, which produces heat. Food more than 4 cm from the surface can only cook by the conduction of this heat from the microwaved area.

Milk

☐ Blending milk and cream into soups and sauces is best done at room temperature. If you are using these from the refrigerator, warm in the microwave on DEFROST (30%) for 30 seconds.

☐ Frozen milk can be thawed easily in the microwave. To thaw, heat the open carton or bottle on DEFROST (30%) for 3–5 minutes. You will need to stir the milk well.

☐ Remember milk is fat-based and tends to boil a little more rapidly than water. It will easily boil over, so when heating milk only fill the dish, cup or jug half full. To be on the safe side use MEDIUM (50–60%) power.

Minced meat

☐ Cook on MEDIUM-HIGH (70%): 500 g will take 10–12 minutes plus 5 minutes' standing time. Cook in a dish that allows fat to drain away.

☐ Defrosting ground beef can be tricky. To avoid cooked lumps, break up the meat and remove any sections that have been defrosted, or shield them with foil. After taking the meat from the oven allow 5 minutes' standing time to complete the defrosting.

☐ To brown ground beef, put it in a plastic colander and stand it over a glass pie dish. Heat for 5–7 minutes per 500 g on HIGH (100%), stirring several times to break up the meat.

Moisture inside oven

☐ Moisture build-up in ovens can vary, but don't forget it depends on the humidity of the day and the type of food cooking.

Muffin pan

☐ The microwave equivalent of a conventional bun tray, which is ideal for patty cakes, fruit pies and baby hamburgers. It is also useful for poached eggs and individual steamed puddings.

Mushrooms

☐ If you wish to bake rather than steam mushrooms, elevate them on a roasting rack.

☐ If you cannot obtain fresh mushrooms, it is better to use dried rather than canned ones, which become mushy with long cooking. To rehydrate dried mushrooms, heat 100 g in 1 cup of water for 5–7 minutes on MEDIUM-LOW (30–40%).

☐ Chopped fresh mushrooms can be used to coat joints of meat before cooking, to give you a good colour and flavour.

☐ To cook fresh mushrooms, wash, slice if desired and put in freezer or oven bag. Secure. Cook on HIGH (100%) for 2–4 minutes for 250 g.

Napkins see **Serviettes**

Noodles see **Pasta**

Nuts

☐ Warm shelled nuts for a few seconds in the microwave before cutting to help bring out the oils for better flavour.

☐ Toast nuts or dried seeds on HIGH (100%), in a single layer on a shallow paper plate. Allow 3–4 minutes per 100 g, stirring during cooking. You can season the nuts or seeds as you wish. Cayenne pepper tossed through makes a good nibble.

O
~~~~

Oats

☐ Try something different for breakfast. Porridge can easily be microwaved.

Odours

☐ If strong smells remain in the oven after cooking, try placing a sprig of rosemary in some water and cook on HIGH (100%) for 2–3 minutes.

☐ After cooking fish, broccoli, etc., bring a cup of water with a good half cup of lemon juice to the boil for a few minutes.

☐ Sometimes new ovens have a certain odour similar to a new burner or a conventional oven – this passes.

Oil

☐ You can reduce or eliminate cooking oil when you are frying in the browning plate in the microwave and sautéing in a dish.

Ongoing cooking see Standing time

Onion

☐ To cook whole onions, peel and place in plastic freezer or oven bag. Secure. Cook on HIGH (100%): 3 onions will take 3–4 minutes.

☐ 1 tablespoon of instant-dried, minced onion is a replacement for 1 small, freshly chopped onion.

☐ Peel onions easily by placing them in a covered container and heating on HIGH (100%) for 1–2 minutes.

Opening door

☐ Unlike a conventional oven, you do not affect the food you are cooking by opening the microwave's door. Make a habit of opening the door to test food, stir and re-start to complete cooking, rather than waiting for the timer to go off and finding the food is overcooked.

Oranges see also Citrus

☐ You can dry orange rind in the microwave by placing it on a paper towel and heating it for 20–30 minutes on DEFROST (30%), stirring frequently. The rind should be very hard after cooling. Stir in an airtight container.

☐ You can reconstitute frozen orange juice concentrate very quickly in the microwave, but remember not to heat it through or you will destroy the Vitamin C.

Outdoor cooking

☐ You can speed up outdoor barbecuing by starting your cooking off in the microwave and then finishing on the barbecue. A great technique, which ensures the meat is cooked on time. Remember you can use your microwave oven to cook wonderful barbecue side dishes like jacket potatoes, corn on the cob and hot potato salad.

Overcooking

☐ This is the biggest problem for beginners, as microwaved food continues cooking when you take it from the oven. To prevent overcooking, you must remember always to under-cook in the first instance. Cooking will be completed during standing time.

P

Paper

☐ Paper is extremely useful for microwave cooking. You can use paper plates, serviettes and towels, and greaseproof paper to cover or wrap food and to absorb moisture and fat.

☐ Paper cups are suitable for making hot drinks, but do not use wax-coated cups as the wax will melt. Similarly, do not use wax-coated plates or dishes.

☐ Do not use recycled paper products in the microwave: they may contain impurities that will cause arcing. Brown paper and newspaper may also contain impurities and should not be used.

☐ Don't use paper towels or serviettes with patterns or colours: the dye may run when it is wet, ruining the food.

☐ If paper has frozen to a box or package, heat on HIGH (100%) for 15 seconds, then stand for 2–3 minutes. You will then be able to remove the paper easily.

☐ Paper towels are invaluable with a microwave oven as they absorb splattering fat and help keep the oven clean. They do not retain the heat or encourage steaming, but they do prevent sogginess. They are ideal for cooking bacon, reheating sandwiches, keeping the surface of bread dry or for covering food that contains enough moisture to be reheated without dehydrating.

Pappadums

☐ To cook pappadums, place three on the outer rim of the turntable and heat on HIGH (100%) for 1 minute. Five pappadums will take 1½ minutes.

Paprika

☐ In conventional cooking paprika is sautéd to release its flavour. With microwaving you can eliminate the fat and microwave a tablespoon of paprika in a small covered glass container on HIGH (100%) for 1½ minutes, shaking several times during the cooking. This will enhance its aroma and colour.

Parsnips

☐ To cook parsnips, peel and chop as desired. Place in plastic oven or freezer bag, secure and cook on HIGH (100%): 500 g will take 6–8 minutes.

Passionfruit

☐ Passionfruit can be frozen in its skin, and you can then defrost on HIGH (100%) when required. One passionfruit take 20–30 seconds.

Pasta

- ☐ To cook pasta or noodles in the microwave use 2 cups of water to 1 cup of pasta, as you would on the stove. Cover the dish.
- ☐ Cooking pasta in the microwave is no faster than on the stove, but it is much cheaper.
- ☐ Add a dash of oil when cooking pasta, to avoid sticking.
- ☐ Pasta should always be drained immediately it comes out of the microwave; it does not require any standing time. It will reheat well on MEDIUM (50–60%): add a knob of butter when reheating.
- ☐ Some noodles cook well in the microwave, others are not so successful. The best are the slim ones, particularly the Chinese and egg noodles and the small shell or spiral pasta. Avoid the larger pasta.
- ☐ Slender noodles will cook more quickly in a microwave than on top of the stove.

Pastry

- ☐ Pastry won't brown in a microwave, so give savoury pastry colour by using a glaze made of egg and Worcestershire sauce, brushed over the shell. Sweet pastry can be coloured by sprinkling a mixture of cinnamon and sugar over the shell.
- ☐ Use wholemeal flour when making pastry, as this will improve the colour.

☐ If you use a clear dish to cook pastry you can check whether or not it is cooked. Pastry won't brown, but when cooked it will be opaque. If it is still transparent it needs more cooking. You can also check for burning – brown spots will appear in the pastry.

☐ **Reheating** pastry is tricky: it goes soggy all too easily. Wrap food in a paper towel or Microcrisp, and elevate on a rack.

☐ Be careful when reheating a fruit pie or tart, as microwaves are attracted to the fruit, so when the pastry feels only warm the filling may be extremely hot.

Patty cakes

☐ Let your batter stand for 10 minutes before microwaving.

☐ Put the same amount of batter into each paper case, or they will cook unevenly.

☐ Patty cakes will rise higher in the microwave than if cooked conventionally, so don't fill the cases as high as usual.

☐ Cook the cakes around the edge of the turntable, or use a muffin pan.

☐ The cakes will still look moist when they are cooked: they will dry as they stand.

Pavlova

☐ Pavlova is best cooked conventionally, but if you try it in the microwave, cook it on a pizza crisper for best results.

Peaches

☐ To peel peaches, lightly slash or prick the skin of the fruit, place on a microwave rack and heat for 30–40 seconds per fruit (the timing will vary with the ripeness, size and firmness of the fruit). You can then remove the skin with a small knife.

☐ To poach peaches, add enough water to cover the fruit and cook for 2–3 minutes on HIGH (100%).

Peas

☐ To cook fresh peas, shell, rinse and put into a plastic freezer or oven bag and secure. Cook on HIGH (100%): 500 g will take 3–5 minutes.

☐ To cook frozen peas, place in a small covered dish with a knob of butter or margarine. Cook on HIGH (100%): 1 cup will take 3–4 minutes.

Petfood

☐ Refrigerated petfood can be warmed in a plastic dish in the microwave on HIGH (100%) for 15–30 seconds, depending on the amount.

Pies see also **Pastry**

☐ Reheating meat pies is most successful if you turn them upside-down on a paper towel or on Microcrisp. Arrange them around the rim of the turntable. The reheating time will depend on how cold the pies are to start with, but averages about 1–1½ minutes per pie on HIGH (100%).

☐ All microwave pie shells need to be blind baked before filling.

☐ Pies are more successful if you don't put a full layer of pastry on top. Try cut-outs or lattice-work.

Pizza

☐ Pizzas are best cooked on a browning dish, although you can buy a special pizza dish if you eat them a lot. Preheat the browning dish for about 5 minutes on HIGH (100%), add a drop of oil, then put your pizza on it for 1 or 2 minutes. This will give a crisp base to the pizza and cook the topping through nicely.

☐ Frozen pizza can be easily defrosted and heated through: one will take 20–30 seconds on HIGH (100%). To prevent the base going soggy, use Microcrisp and elevate the pizza.

Placement see also **Arranging food in oven**

☐ Make sure you put thick, dense portions of food towards the outer rim of the turntable or dish, where they will cook more quickly.

☐ If you are cooking a number of similar-sized items, place them around the edge of the turntable, with space between each.

☐ If you are cooking a casserole, or something similar, make sure you stir the dish 2–3 times through cooking.

☐ If you can't stir, because it is something like a layered potato dish, elevate the dish on a roasting rack so that all parts get equal microwaves distribution.

Plastic

☐ Plastic is widely used in microwave cooking, in the form of bags, cookware and wrap.

☐ When buying plastic cookware, choose dishes that have a high heat resistance (180°C and over); have rounded corners for even cooking; are freezer-safe, so you can take meals from the freezer and put them straight into the microwave; and for your own convenience, that can go in the dishwasher.

☐ Avoid very cheap plastic cookware, as you may find that it is only suitable for reheating or cooking on low power.

☐ Do not attempt to cook food with a high fat or sugar content, such as roast meats, bacon or confectionery, unless you are sure the dish is resistant to high heat. Otherwise it will melt.

☐ Do not use plasticware such as Melamine or Tupperware in the microwave. They absorb microwaves and food does not cook in them.

☐ Do not use ice-cream or margarine containers in the microwave.

☐ Plastic takeaway containers are not suitable for cooking raw food, only for reheating. They will warp and melt.

☐ Oven bags are safe for microwave cooking. They can go in the freezer, are ideal for marinating and then cooking, keep the oven clean, and ensure all the flavour and goodness of the food is retained. The bag should be vented by pricking holes in it before cooking. Never use metal twist ties to secure the oven bag: instead use a rubber band, piece of string, or tear a piece of plastic from the top of the bag and use it as a tie. Freezer bags can also be used in the microwave.

☐ Plastic wrap is not always suitable for use in the microwave. Always check the brand you buy is recommended for microwave cooking. If the packet is not marked as suitable for microwave cooking the wrap may melt at high temperatures.

Platestackers

☐ If you want to reheat two plates at a time you will find a platestacker a handy item of microware. However microwave ovens are designed to cook a single layer.

Playdough

☐ If your children have produced playdough work that you want to keep, dry it in the microwave oven, on a paper towel, on DEFROST (30%) for about 1½ minutes per piece, turning half-way through. When they are cool the sculptures can be painted.

Plums

☐ Fresh plums can be peeled more easily by heating on HIGH (100%) for ½–1 minute, and then being allowed to stand for 2 or 3 minutes.

Poaching

☐ The microwave oven is ideal for poaching food. Eggs, fruit, meat, fish, poultry and seafood can all be cooked very successfully.

☐ Make sure the poaching liquid covers all the food, or exposed portions will be overcooked.

Popcorn

☐ Popcorn is simple to make in the microwave oven: take a large dish with a cover and put a generous handful of corn into it. Add a small teaspoon of water or oil, cover the dish and cook on HIGH (100%) for 4–5 minutes.

☐ If you are a keen popcorn-eater, you can obtain a special microwave-safe corn popper. Listen for the popping to slow down. This is a sign to remove the dish from the oven.

☐ Jazz up your popcorn: make up a savoury mix with 2 teaspoons celery salt, 2 teaspoons paprika, 1 teaspoon onion salt and ½ teaspoon cayenne. Then just sprinkle it through the hot corn.

Pork see also Meat

☐ When **roasting** loin, leg or shoulder of pork, cook with the skin-side down first and turn over half-way through.

☐ Don't cook a pork joint in an oven bag. Pork needs to dry out slightly as it cooks, and a bag tends to give a steamed result.

☐ To cook a joint of pork, score the skin, then cook on MEDIUM-HIGH (70%). A loin will take 8–10 minutes per 500 g.

☐ While the joint is standing, cook the crackling (it won't cook enough while the meat is in the oven). After the meat is cooked, remove the rind, brush with oil and sprinkle with salt, cut it into pieces and put it on absorbent paper towels. Cover with a double layer of towels. Cook on a rack on HIGH (100%) for 2 minutes at a time until the crackling is really crisp. It will still be rather pale, though, and not conventionally brown.

☐ To cook **pork chops**, place bone ends towards the oven's centre and elevate on a roasting rack. Cook on MEDIUM (50%):

1 chop will take 4–5 minutes with 3 minutes' standing time;
2 chops will take 5–6 minutes with 3 minutes' standing time;
4 chops will take 6–7 minutes with 4 minutes' standing time.

Porridge see Oats

Potatoes

☐ When cooking potatoes in their jackets, always pierce the skin before cooking to prevent bursting. Place on a paper towel, arrange round the rim of the turntable and cook on HIGH (100%): 1 medium potato will take 3–4 minutes; 2 will take 4–5 minutes; 4 will take 8–10 minutes. Much faster than baking them in the oven! After cooking wrap potatoes in foil and allow to stand 5–10 minutes.

☐ To cook peeled potatoes, wash and cut them if desired. Put in a plastic bag, secure and cook on HIGH (100%): 500 g will take 8–10 minutes.

☐ Mashed potatoes will reheat best if you press the centre down, thus forming an outer ring.

Pot pourri

☐ Spread fresh petals and fragrant leaves on paper towels and remove stems. Sprinkle them all over with orris root – 1 tablespoon to 1 cup petals. Cover petals with a paper towel, microwave on HIGH (100%): the exact time will depend on the amount of flowers and their type, but is in the order of 30 seconds to 2½ minutes. Check frequently. When dry add grated nutmeg, citrus rind, crushed coriander seeds, cloves, cinnamon stick and vanilla stick, to your liking.

Poultry

☐ Turkey should be cooked on MEDIUM (50%) for 15–18 minutes per 500 g, with a standing time of 35 minutes.

☐ All other poultry can be cooked on MEDIUM-HIGH (70%): chicken for 8–9 minutes per 500 g, with a standing time of 20 minutes; duck for 8–10 minutes per 500 g, with a standing time of 20 minutes.

☐ If the bird is stuffed, add 1 minute extra for each 500 g weight of bird after stuffing.

☐ In addition to the standing time at the end, poultry is improved if you give it 15 minutes' standing time half-way through cooking.

☐ For tender and juicy results, you can also cook poultry on MEDIUM (50%). It will take a little longer.

☐ Always pierce the skin of poultry before cooking in the microwave to allow the steam to escape and prevent loud popping noises.

☐ To help the appearance and colour of poultry you can pour boiling water over the bird after the skin has been pierced. You can also brush a mixture of brown sugar and honey mixed with a little soy sauce over the bird half-way through the cooking time.

☐ Save any bones from your bird and freeze them. You can then defrost them quickly in the microwave when you want to make a stock or soup.

☐ Poultry should be roasted in a heat-resistant, non-metallic baking dish, raised on a roasting rack so that it is fat-free. A whole bird should be started with the breast-side down and turned over half-way through the cooking. Poultry may be basted with melted butter and covered with wax paper or paper towels to prevent splattering.

☐ All frozen poultry should be completely defrosted, washed, dried and allowed to stand at room temperature for an hour before cooking.

☐ You can freeze chicken or turkey parts and thaw in your microwave on DEFROST (30%) for 7–10 minutes per 500 g.

☐ You no longer have to wait for chicken or turkey leftovers to make your favourite salad or casserole. You can microwave a few chicken or turkey fillets on MEDIUM (50%) for 10 minutes per 500 g, cool and remove any skin and bone.

Power see also Wattage

☐ It is important to know the maximum power output of your microwave oven. Most ovens are 700–900 watts, but some

have outputs of only 500 watts, and food will cook slower in
these. Most recipes are given for ovens with higher power
output, so if you have a smaller one you will have to amend
the recipe, lengthening the cooking time.

☐ You can vary the power output of your oven by using the
controls. Most ovens have a series of graduated power settings. These may be marked 1 through to 10, or in percent-
ages of full power, or by designated names. The chart below
gives the equivalent percentage power of each setting, with
an indication of what cooking is done at these power levels.

Setting	Percentage power	Cooking purpose
Low	10–20%	warm
Defrost	30–35%	defrost
Medium-low	30–40%	simmer
Medium	50–60%	poach, bake
Medium-high	70–80%	roast, reheat
High	100%	sauté, boil, steam

☐ On HIGH power the microwaves enter the oven 100% of the
time; on LOW they enter for 10–20% of the cycle, and stop for
the rest of the time.

Prawns
☐ Prawns are cooked when they turn opaque. Be careful not to
overcook them – they will become rubbery very quickly.

Preserves see **Jams, jellies and chutneys**

Pricking

☐ Pricking is much used in microwave cookery. All food with a membrane or skin should be pricked – for instance, jacket potatoes, poached egg yolks, sausages, baked apples, liver and kidney. Food should never be cooked in a completely sealed container, such as a plastic bag. Always prick the bag to allow steam to escape, or the bag will burst.

Pulses

☐ To speed up the cooking of dried peas and other pulses, rather than soaking them overnight, you can cover them with cold water, bring them to the boil on HIGH (100%) for about 10 minutes, then simmer on DEFROST (30%) for 30–40 minutes. They will then be ready to use.

Pumpkin

☐ Heat pumpkin in the microwave on HIGH (100%) for 1–2 minutes to soften and make it easy to chop.

☐ To cook pumpkin, peel and chop. Place in freezer or oven bag and secure. Cook on HIGH (100%): 500 g will take 8–10 minutes.

☐ You can turn the seeds of a pumpkin into a snack to have with drinks. Scoop out the seeds from the pumpkin, wash and dry well. Lay on baking paper on a plate and cook on HIGH (100%) for about 5 minutes, stirring several times during the cooking and watching that they do not burn. When they are dried, season with curry powder, cumin or chilli powder and stand for 5 minutes.

Q

Quantity

☐ Whatever quantity of food is placed in the microwave oven to cook, the amount of microwave energy available to cook it remains the same. When increasing the quantities of food for defrosting, heating or cooking, therefore, the length of cooking time also needs to be increased proportionately. Allow about half as much time again when doubling the amount of food, and decrease the cooking time by one-third when halving the quantities.

☐ Because small amounts cook and heat through faster than larger quantities, it is more efficient to cook in two batches rather than overfill one large dish.

Quiches

☐ Quiches can be made very successfully in the microwave because there is no possibility of them burning or becoming lumpy.

☐ Ensure ingredients are at room temperature before mixing.

☐ If the outer edges are looking cooked before the centre is ready, shield them with foil.

R

Radiation

☐ There has never been any type of injury from microwave radiation in Australia. It is an extremely safe form of cooking. As soon as the door opens the microwaves are immediately cut off. There is no residual radiation in the food, and it is safe to eat immediately it comes out of the oven. Looking through the door cannot hurt one's eyes, nor can men become sterile from microwave cooking!

Raisins see **Dried fruit**

Reheating

☐ Reheating cooked dishes (or heating up leftovers) is one of the biggest advantages of microwave cooking. Quick, easy and efficient reheating carries the extra advantage of no loss of quality in taste or texture. Food tastes freshly cooked, not tired and warmed over, as is frequently the case with a conventional oven – and many of the better restaurants are using microwaves in this way now.

☐ Do not overdo reheating. Monitoring the internal temperature of the food is important: if you have a probe in your machine you can check the internal temperature of the food; if not, use a food thermometer.

☐ To avoid overcooking, use variable cooking power: We

suggest MEDIUM-HIGH or MEDIUM, which is about 70% or 50% microwave power.

☐ Starting temperature of the food is important. Refrigerated food will take longer than food at room temperature.

☐ Moisture is also important. Some dishes, for example casseroles or rice, absorb all liquid during the first cooking, so add 2 or 3 tablespoons of water, stock or wine, or a pat of butter before reheating. Moisture and fat attract energy and will reheat the food more evenly.

☐ The food is ready to eat when it transfers enough heat to the dish to warm it, and when some moisture is visible on the cover.

☐ You can reheat **soup** in a tureen or in a mug, but always stir at least once.

☐ **Stews** should be covered and stirred several times during cooking time. Reheat on MEDIUM (50–60%).

☐ Never reheat **meat or poultry** on HIGH, or it will toughen. Thin slices of meat will reheat more evenly and quickly than thick or irregular pieces. Reheat sliced meat topped with a gravy or sauce to add moisture, and cover with waxed paper or plastic wrap. To reheat chops, fillets or chicken pieces, arrange on the baking dish with the thicker portion towards the outside of the dish. Bones conduct the heat, so watch carefully. Reheat on MEDIUM (50–60%).

☐ **Vegetables** with a sauce or those that have been puréed reheat especially well. Always cover the dish and stir several times; use a MEDIUM (50–60%) power. To reheat fresh vegetables, first cover with plastic film to retain moisture. You can arrange the vegetables on a microwave rack if you wish to avoid steaming.

☐ **Cakes, pastry, muffins and bread** are tricky to reheat. Too much reheating can make even the most tender baked food as hard as a rock. Bread slices, rolls and muffins take only 10–15 seconds on HIGH (100%), 15–25 seconds if frozen. Arrange on a microwave rack or a paper towel to help absorb the moisture. Sugar sprinkled on a slice of cake will attract energy, as will the fruit filling in pies, although the crust may remain relatively cool. Pastry can become soggy when reheated.

☐ **Desserts** are easy to reheat. For 1 serve, heat on MEDIUM-HIGH (70%) for 30–60 seconds, depending on the type of dessert: a heavy crumble will take longer than a light sponge. Whole desserts are best heated on MEDIUM (50–60%) for 1–3 minutes per serve.

☐ Dishes that cannot be stirred (such as lasagne) should be reheated on DEFROST (30–40%) power, so that the cheese and meat do not toughen and the pasta remains moist.

☐ Individual servings reheat successfully, but carve the meat into thin slices, cover with sauce or gravy and choose vegetables of uniform size and density, e.g. peas and carrots, or beans and broccoli, so they heat at the same time. Cover the plate with plastic wrap.

☐ **Jacket potatoes** dehydrate quickly if overcooked, so wrap them in plastic wrap before reheating.

☐ Egg and cheese dishes can separate on reheating, so use DEFROST (30%) and stir frequently.

Rice

☐ To serve 5 to 6 people, use 300 g of rice and cook for 25 minutes on DEFROST (30–40%). To serve 7 to 8 people, use 400 g of rice and cook for 30 minutes on DEFROST. Always use twice as much luke-warm water as rice. Cook uncovered. Stand for 5 minutes.

☐ Cooking rice in a microwave oven takes almost as long as on the top of the stove, but it always cooks well and you can serve the rice in the container it cooks in. Always rinse rice under cold water before cooking. Toss the cooked rice gently to prevent mushiness.

☐ Rice freezes well. Keep small quantities of leftover rice in the freezer to defrost and add to recipes.

☐ When mixing rice, a hard-fibred food, with soft-fibred foods, such as in a paella, risotto or Chinese dish, the rice should be cooked so that the finished dish cooks quickly and evenly.

☐ For fluffy white rice, add ½ teaspoon of lemon juice to 500 ml water and cook 200 g rice in this. The lemon water will give the rice a nice finish.

☐ Always reheat rice with a tablespoon of water, wine, stock or a knob of butter to prevent it drying out.

Rind

☐ You can dry lemon or orange rind by placing the grated rind (not the white membranes) on several pieces of paper towel and heating for 2–3 minutes on HIGH (100%), or on DEFROST (30%) for 20–30 minutes, rearranging the rind frequently during the cooking time. The rind should be very hard after cooling and can be stored in an airtight container.

Rissoles see Burgers

Roasting see also Beef, Lamb, Meat, Pork, Poultry, Veal

☐ Roasting is generally most successful at MEDIUM (50–60%) or MEDIUM-HIGH (70–80%). If you cook on HIGH (100%) the meat can toughen.

☐ Shield the ends of large joints half-way through cooking.

☐ The meat will not colour as in conventional cooking, so you will have to test doneness by piercing the meat and looking at the colour of the juices.

☐ **Open roasting** is suitable for cuts such as rolled, boned rib of beef, leg of lamb, loin and leg of pork, and poultry. Place meat fat side down on a roasting rack, in an ovenproof dish, and cover with a piece of kitchen paper to absorb splatters. Turn meat over half-way through cooking. Allow standing time.

☐ **Oven-bag roasting** is suitable for leaner cuts, such as veal joints, beef sirloin, pork loin and leg and poultry. Place meat in bag on roasting rack and stand in an ovenproof dish. Turn meat over half-way through cooking. Remove from bag for standing.

□ **Pot roasting** is suitable for tougher cuts of meat, such as top-side and brisket of beef and forequarter of lamb. Ensure lid fits well, and cook meat in a minimal amount of liquid. Cook on MEDIUM-HIGH (70%) for 5 minutes and then complete cooking on DEFROST (30–40%).

Roasting rack

□ Used to elevate food for more even cooking or defrosting. Possibly the most useful utensil in microwave cooking.

Rotating antenna

□ This is fitted in either the base or roof of some ovens, and it diverts the microwaves around the oven to prevent hot and cold spots.

Rubber bands

□ Use rubber bands instead of metal tie twists to secure plastic bags for use in the microwave.

S

Safety

□ Microwave ovens are extremely safe. Because they don't get hot you can't burn yourself while using them.

□ The microwaves are contained within the oven and can't cause any damage. If you are at all worried that micro-waves might be escaping from your oven – for instance, if the door seems loose – have it checked by the maker's service agent.

☐ Never attempt to mend your microwave yourself. If the oven has been damaged or broken, ensure it is repaired by a qualified technician.

☐ If microwave ovens are operated empty they can be damaged. Many microwave ovens are now fitted with a child lock – check your manual.

Salt

☐ Never add salt to food you are going to cook in the microwave: it makes it tough by drawing the water to the surface, where it quickly evaporates. Salt also discolours the food surfaces.

Sandwiches

☐ Day-old bread, which has lost some of its moisture, is best for sandwiches. A regular complaint about heating sandwiches in the microwave is that they become soggy on the bottom. If you are heating sandwiches, place on a paper towel to absorb excess moisture, or on a roasting rack. Toasted bread doesn't become so soggy.

☐ Tomato sauce or pickles should be added after the sandwich is heated.

☐ The edges of the filling should be higher or bulkier than the centre to ensure even heating.

☐ Fillings absorb more energy and become hotter than the bread, so allow to stand a few minutes before eating.

☐ Toasted sandwiches can be cooked on the browning plate. Preheat plate for 3–4 minutes on HIGH (100%), and place your buttered sandwich on the hot dish. Flatten it with a spatula and turn after 15–20 seconds. The second side might take 30–35 seconds.

☐ Sandwiches can be heated in paper bags, as can hot dogs.

☐ Sandwiches with cheese: place the cheese in the centre of the sandwich or add cheese 30 seconds before the end of cooking, or it will become stringy and overcooked.

☐ Sandwiches with a meat filling: the sandwich will heat faster if the meat is thinly sliced.

Saucepans see also **Casserole dishes**

☐ In the microwave oven you use casserole dishes instead of traditional saucepans with handles.

Sauces

☐ Cornflour is low in gluten and will give a smoother finish than flour.

☐ Stir sauces at least once, bringing the outside to the centre and the less-cooked centre part to the outside of the dish. This will ensure that your sauce is smooth and even-textured.

☐ Prevent boil-overs by using a container double the volume of the ingredients.

☐ If your white sauce is overcooked and a thick blob, whirl it briefly in the blender or food processor – no one will know and even the best chefs have done this at times!

☐ If the ingredients of the sauce have come straight out of the refrigerator, remember that the cooking time will be a little longer.

☐ Remember sauces that are made with unsalted butter are the most successful. Margarine has a large quantity of water in it, which affects the end result of the sauce; it is not recommended.

☐ Sauces that become too thick are better if thinned with wine, water or stock then milk and should be stirred well before reheating.

☐ The absence of direct heat in the microwave means that sauces do not reduce as much as with stove-top cooking, so less fluid is needed.

☐ You can measure, mix and cook sauces in the same cup or jug. A measuring jug is the most convenient container.

☐ Basic white sauces can be cooked on HIGH (100%). Sauces containing eggs or cheese should be cooked on DEFROST (30–40%).

☐ When making sauces for casseroles or puddings, you may need to add a little more thickening agent to counteract the lack of reduction.

☐ You can make a quantity of sauce and freeze what is not used. Reheat the sauce on DEFROST (30–40%): 250 ml of sauce will take a minute or two to warm through.

☐ To use up the last drops of tomato sauce or mayonnaise add 1 tablespoon of orange and lemon juice, red wine or butter

to the bottle. Heat for 45 seconds and give the bottle a good shake.
- [ ] To make tomato or chilli sauce easier to pour, heat the bottle for 15 seconds on HIGH (100%).

Sausages
- [ ] Prick the skins of sausages before cooking.
- [ ] Thick sausages: 2 will take 3–4 minutes on MEDIUM-HIGH (70%), with 2 minutes' standing time; 4 will take 6 minutes, with 3 minutes' standing time.
- [ ] Thin sausages: 2 will take 3 minutes on MEDIUM-HIGH (70%), with 2 minutes' standing time; 4 will take 5 minutes, with 3 minutes' standing time.

Scallops
- [ ] Never overcook scallops, or they will become like little rubber balls. Cook on MEDIUM (50–60%) – 500 g will take 4 minutes – and let them stand in their juices to complete cooking.

Seafood see Fish, Shellfish

Seeds
- [ ] Sesame seeds and poppy seeds can be toasted easily in the microwave oven. Cook on HIGH (100%) on a plate, without butter or oil, but keep moving them about. Try toasting them in an oven bag: it is far easier to shake around.

Sensor see Temperature probe

Serviettes

☐ Serviettes can be used to wrap food during microwave cooking, so long as they are cotton or linen. Material containing synthetic fibres should not be used.

☐ Stale bread can be refreshed by wrapping a damp serviette around it and heating for a few seconds.

Servings

☐ Servings can be heated directly on plates to simplify life for a busy cook. Always cover plates when heating.

Shapes

☐ Shapes of dishes are important in the microwave: choose dishes with rounded corners; ring casseroles or loops are the best shape for microwave penetration; a large, flat and shallow dish will cook the same amount of food faster than a deep dish.

☐ Shapes of food are equally important: aim for uniform pieces of food. Cut your meat and vegetables to uniform size, or you will find some pieces are cooked while others are not. If the food can't be made into an even shape, e.g. a chicken drumstick, put the thick part towards the edge of the turntable, and shield the thinner end with foil if necessary.

☐ Food will cook more rapidly in the microwave oven if you cut it into smaller pieces.

Shellfish see also Prawns, Scallops

☐ Cooking shellfish is the same whether it is in or out of the shell; the power and cooking times do not alter.

☐ Shellfish can be steamed in their shells. Cook 12 mussels or oysters on MEDIUM (50–60%) for 3–4 minutes or until the shells partly open. Anything that does not open is bad, so throw it out. These are delicious served with melted butter and lemon.

☐ For those of you who like to freeze lobster tails and have them ready for special occasions, remember they are very delicate. Defrosting before heating is required only for a full-sized or thick tail.

Arrange thick lobster tails in a shallow dish, spreading them out, and microwave on DEFROST (30%) for about 3–5 minutes per 500 g. Remove the tails when they are still a little bit icy and run under cool water.

It isn't necessary to defrost small lobster tails – 4 cm thick or less – just wash and wrap them in plastic wrap, place them spoke-shape around your turntable, with the thicker ends on the outside, and microwave direct on MEDIUM (50%) for 4–5 minutes per 500 g. If the tails curl up tightly, you've overcooked!

Shielding see also **Aluminium foil**
☐ Use foil to shield areas of food – corners, ends, thin areas – that might otherwise become overcooked.

Skewers see also **Toothpicks**
☐ Use wooden skewers in the microwave oven as metal ones may cause arcing.

Skin tonic

☐ Herbal skin tonics are easily prepared in the microwave. Make a simple infusion by adding 2 tablespoons of herb to a cup of water and bringing to the boil in the oven. Allow to stand for 2–3 minutes to cool before using. Herbs that are good for skins include fennel, parsley and sage. Sage tonic is astringent and particularly good for oily skins.

Slices see also **Biscuits, Cakes**

☐ In the microwave slices are best cooked in a round or square dish. Traditional rectangular slice dishes will cook the slice unevenly, so the sides are overcooked before the centre is ready.

Slimmers

☐ Microwave cooking is ideal for slimmers as it is fat- and salt-free in most instances. Instead of salt you can add herbs and spices to give flavour.

Snacks

☐ For a quick bite, cut a small piece of cheese and put it on a cracker biscuit. Pop it in the microwave for 15–20 seconds on HIGH (100%). Delicious.

Soap

☐ If you find yourself with little piece of soap when the cake is almost finished, place several of them in the microwave for 1–2 minutes on HIGH (100%) with a cup of water separately. The soap will soften and you can then mould the pieces together into a ball, and you've got a new little cake of soap for the handbasin!

Softening

☐ Soften **honey** that has crystallised in the jar. You will be able to get the last drop from the bottom. Use MEDIUM (50–60%) power.

☐ Add an apple wedge to **brown sugar**, cover and heat on HIGH (100%) for 45 seconds.

☐ Soften **cheeses** that are best served at room temperature. You can heat these for the short time necessary on wooden cheese serving dishes. Use DEFROST (30–40%) power.

☐ Heat **dessert sauces** for a very special touch on HIGH (100%).

☐ **Ice-cream** can be brought to serving consistency after 30–60 seconds in the microwave on DEFROST (30%).

☐ If you keep **peanut butter** in the refrigerator it will become spreadable after just seconds in the microwave oven, but remove the metal lid before heating.

☐ Block **cream** or **cottage cheese** can be softened for recipes or spreading – make sure you remove the foil wrapper first and use DEFROST (30–40%) at 15-second intervals.

Soufflé

☐ Soufflés don't cook successfully in the microwave because they won't form a crust.

Soup

☐ Soup can be heated in the container you are going to serve it in. One decent-sized mug or bowl of soup will take 2 or 3 minutes: multiply by the number of mugs that you are intending to serve.

☐ Soups that make popping sounds? Stir the soup several times and then set your power a little lower . . . this will stop the popping.

☐ If you are making soup from scratch, make sure you use a large enough bowl so the soup doesn't boil over.

☐ Water or stock-based home-made soups are cooked with a cover, and milk-based soups without a cover. Remember, milk tends to boil more rapidly than water.

☐ Soup stock can be frozen in containers or ice-cube trays and defrosted in your microwave to add to casseroles as required.

☐ Use HIGH (100%) power for heating tomato or broth-based soups. Delicate soups like creamy asparagus soup should be done on MEDIUM (50–60%) or even a DEFROST setting (30%).

☐ **Canned soups** should be put in a bowl with the required milk or water and covered for best results: 250 ml of canned soup will heat in 3 or 4 minutes; 1 litre will take 8 to 9 minutes.

☐ Soups are an ideal way to introduce new foods to your family. Children who will not eat a vegetable such as pumpkin will often happily eat pumpkin soup.

Spices see also **Herbs**

☐ The short cooking time in a microwave oven highlights the flavour of spices in food, therefore adjust the seasoning to your taste after cooking.

☐ Spices and herbs should be added at the beginning of microwave cooking, not towards the end.

☐ Enliven old, tired spices by placing them in the microwave and heating for 45 seconds on HIGH (100%) before using them in dishes.

☐ Place whole spices in small muslin bags or cloths so that you can remove them easily from a dish when you have achieved the desired flavour.

Spinach

☐ To cook fresh spinach, chop as desired, rinse and put in plastic freezer or oven bag. Cook on HIGH (100%): 250 g will take 2–4 minutes.

☐ To wilt a bunch of spinach, wash it well and cut into ribbons. Place in a microwave-safe bag and heat on HIGH for 30–60 seconds only.

☐ Defrost frozen spinach quickly on MEDIUM (50%) for 5–7 minutes.

Sponge cakes

☐ Sponges should be cooked in a plastic, microwave-safe, 2-litre casserole dish.

☐ Sponges are ideal cakes to make in the microwave as they do not require browning.

Squash

☐ To cook a small squash, rinse, prick and place whole in plastic freezer or oven bag. Secure. Cook on HIGH (100%): 500 g will take 4–5 minutes.

☐ Squash, like potatoes, can be cooked whole without a covering. Always prick them in several places to prevent popping.

Standing time

☐ After food has been removed from a microwave oven it will continue to cook because of conduction of heat within the food. It is important to take care not to overcook food and to allow this standing time.

☐ Always cook food for the minimum time given in the recipe, then test for doneness *after* standing time. If the food is not quite ready, cook a little longer.

☐ Cover food with foil or a lid during standing time, to retain heat.

☐ Standing time is essential for meat and poultry. Their internal temperature will increase by as much as 6°C during standing time.

☐ Cakes and egg dishes must be removed from the oven while still moist and not quite cooked, and left to 'set' during standing time.

Starting temperature

☐ If food comes straight from the fridge into the microwave, it's going to take a minute or two longer to cook than food at room temperature: the exact time will depend on the quantity of food.

Steak see also **Beef**

☐ Steak can be cooked in your microwave if you have no other cooking appliance; however the microwave is not the best method for cooking steaks. As the cooking time is so quick the meat often ends up tough and pale in colour.

☐ Steaks are best marinated and cooked in a casserole-style recipe. Partially cook the vegetables first.

☐ When cooking steak always use MEDIUM (50–60%); it may take a few minutes longer but the end result will be worth waiting for.

Steamed puddings

☐ Steamed puddings are delicious, especially in winter, but they can take hours to cook on the stove. In the microwave a steamed pudding can cook in 4–5 *minutes*, depending on the recipe.

☐ Cook the pudding covered for the first stage, and for the last few minutes remove the cover to prevent the pudding becoming too heavy and steamed.

Stews see **Casseroles**

Stir-frying

☐ You can stir-fry in the microwave in a browning dish or frying skillet. Stir-frying in the microwave uses less oil than on the stove top.

Stirring and turning

☐ Because microwaves only penetrate about 4 cm into the food, for even results it is necessary to stir food so that the centre cooks. Food which cannot be stirred – for instance bread and cakes – must be elevated instead. Meat should be turned over half-way through cooking.

☐ Sauces must be stirred during cooking to prevent lumps.

Stock see also Soup

☐ You can make a quick stock by cooking meat or poultry bones and scraps in the microwave with some water. For each 500 ml water allow 5 minutes' cooking time on HIGH (100%) and a further 10 minutes on DEFROST (30–40%). Stand for several minutes and then strain.

☐ Using hot stock will speed up the cooking time of any soup.

Sugar

☐ Use castor sugar in the microwave, as its fine texture means that it cooks more quickly.

☐ To soften hard brown sugar, add a slice of white bread or an apple wedge to 1 cup sugar and heat, covered, on HIGH (100%) for 45–50 seconds.

Sultanas see **Dried fruit**

Sweet potato

☐ There are two varieties of sweet potato (also known as yam): one is potato-coloured, the other is a pale pumpkin colour. We prefer the latter as the colour is more appealing after cooking in the microwave.

☐ Cook sweet potato as you would potato baked in its jacket: scrub, pierce the skin and place around the turntable on a paper towel. Sweet potatoes should be uniform in size and shape for even cooking. Microwave on HIGH (100%): 1 medium sweet potato will take 3–4 minutes, 500 g will take 6–8 minutes. Turn sweet potatoes over half-way through cooking.

☐ Always allow to stand 3–5 minutes to complete the cooking.

Sweetcorn

☐ Sweetcorn is delicious cooked on the cob in the microwave. If the leaves have been removed, wrap individually in plastic wrap. If the leaves are present, cook them as they are. Cook on HIGH (100%): one cob will take 3–4 minutes.

☐ When cooking sweetcorn in its jacket, you can pull the leaves back before cooking and rub the corn with garlic or herbs, then butter, and re-cover with the leaves.

Sweets

☐ Sugar syrup boils at a very high temperature, so ensure that the cooking dish you use is of good quality and can withstand these high temperatures. Sugar syrups increase in volume when they boil, so use a large enough dish.

☐ Chocolate or milk-based sweets should be cooked on low power settings: DEFROST (30%). Chocolate may burn if cooked at too high a power.

☐ Marshmallows and caramels can be softened enough to blend with other ingredients by cooking on HIGH (100%) for 30–60 seconds.

T

Tea

☐ Don't boil tea in the microwave because it tends to stew. But you can still make tea: put a mug or cup of cold water in the oven, add a teabag, and heat on HIGH (100%) for 2 minutes. The water should just boil, and you have a cup of tea!

Temperature

☐ Remember that the colder the food is when you put it in the microwave oven the longer it will take to cook. Always allow for this in timing.

Temperature probe

☐ A temperature probe is supplied with some microwave ovens: one end is inserted into the food and the other into the oven. The oven can then be programmed to cook until the required internal temperature of the food is reached, when it will turn itself off. The probe is sometimes called a sensor.

Tenting
☐ Tenting is when paper towels, greaseproof paper or baking parchment are folded into a tent-shape over the food that is cooking.

Texture of food
☐ Microwaves can penetrate light, porous food more easily than dense, heavy, tight-fibred food. This is why bread and cakes cook so much faster than meat or heavier vegetables such as potatoes.

Thermometers
☐ You can't cook with a conventional thermometer in the microwave oven, because it's made of metal, but special microwave thermometers are available. If you are using a conventional meat thermometer to check the temperature of the joint or bird, remember to wait about 5 minutes to allow the thermometer to reach the correct temperature. When making jam or sweets you will probably have to rely on a conventional sugar thermometer, but as it's metal remember that it cannot be used while the microwave oven is operating.

Thickening see Cornflour

Timing see also Cooking times
☐ Exact timing of any recipe depends on many variables: the

size and shape of the food to be cooked; the temperature; the amount of fat and sugar in it; and how moist it is. Different ovens, with slightly different power outputs, will also affect the length of cooking time. When in doubt, always *under-cook*, then allow standing time before checking to see if the dish is ready. If it isn't, pop it back into the oven.

Toast see also **Sandwiches**

☐ Toast can be reheated by microwaving on HIGH (100%) for 20–25 seconds per slice.

Tomato

☐ Place whole tomatoes on a small plate, prick and cook uncovered on HIGH (100%). One tomato will take 1–2 minutes.

☐ To peel a tomato, prick the skin lightly with a fork, elevate on a roasting rack and heat for 45 seconds on HIGH (100%). Stand for 5 minutes, then peel.

☐ Tomato sauce can be warmed to make it a pouring consistency. Take off metal lid and warm bottle for 30–60 seconds.

Toothpicks see also **Skewers**

☐ Toothpicks can be used in the microwave oven, but only use wooden ones. Plastic toothpicks will melt during cooking.

Toppings

☐ Since microwaved foods are often pale, toppings can improve their attractiveness. For savoury foods try combinations of toasted breadcrumbs with cheese and melted butter, or breadcrumbs with finely chopped bacon or herbs. Mashed potatoes can be topped with tomatoes and Parmesan cheese. Any topping that is just cheese, or has a large amount of cheese in it, should be added towards the end of cooking otherwise the cheese will overcook and become tough.

☐ Shredded cheese mixed with paprika can be sprinkled over ground meat or meatloaf after cooking is completed.

☐ For fruit puddings top with a crumble topping, made with wholemeal flour and brown sugar, for extra colour. Alternatively try a topping of crushed ginger biscuits and brown sugar. Chocolate and caramel sauces can also be used for dessert toppings.

☐ Top drinks that have been heated in the microwave with a special cream. To whipped cream add some icing sugar and a little liqueur or spirit, or flavour extract, plus one or more of the following if appropriate: citrus rind, chocolate curls, nutmeg or cinnamon.

Toughness

☐ Tough or dry food is usually an indication of overcooking: either cooking for too long, or at too high a power setting. Once it's overdone there is no remedy.

Towels

☐ Produce hot, steamy towels by wetting face flannels, squeezing them dry and putting them in the microwave under plastic wrap; heat for 45 seconds each on HIGH (100%). The hot towel makes a good compress for aching muscles, and is a treat for a man at the end of a shave, sprinkled with a little cologne. After a dinner party you can give your guests a hot towel each with a little rose essence sprinkled over.

Turkey see also Poultry

☐ When defrosting a turkey, do not leave it out overnight as the surface will warm up long before the interior has thawed. Defrost in the bottom of your refrigerator or use the microwave on DEFROST (30%), weighing the bird carefully and timing accordingly.

☐ To roast a turkey successfully, use MEDIUM-HIGH (70%) for 10 minutes, then reduce to MEDIUM (50–60%). Turkeys up to size 40, but no larger, are best for microwaving.

☐ Calculate the cooking time on the weight after stuffing. With a turkey up to size 40, turn between 3 and 4 times during cooking. Drain off excess fats and juices as they accumulate, as this will help to shorten the cooking time and prevent spattering.

☐ Leftover turkey can be frozen. If it is without gravy, use within 1 month of freezing; if covered with a sauce or in a casserole, you can keep it for up to 6 months.

☐ Shield the wing tips and drumstick ends of turkey half-way through cooking to prevent overcooking.

☐ Wiggle the thigh joint to test for doneness – it should move easily – and the juices should run clear. After removing from the oven cover with foil and allow to stand for at least 15 minutes.

Turnip

☐ To cook, peel and chop as desired. Place in freezer or oven bag and secure. Cook on HIGH (100%): 500 g will take 6–8 minutes.

Turntable

☐ The turntable ensures even cooking. It elevates the cooking dish off the floor of the oven and keeps the food moving through the pattern of microwaves, helping to eliminate cold spots.

U

Utensils see also **Dishes, Equipment, Plastic,** individual dishes

☐ To test if a particular dish is suitable for microwave use, put it in the oven next to a measuring jug containing 120 ml of cold water. Run the oven on HIGH (100%) for 1 minute. If the water is warm and the dish cool, it may be used for microwave cooking. If both are warm, use the dish only for reheating. If the dish gets hot, while the water stays cool, do *not* use the dish in your oven.

☐ Shape of a dish is very important. Round dishes, ring casseroles and loops are the best for microwave penetration, which is about 4 cm into the food.

☐ A shallow dish will cook the same amount of food faster than a deep dish, as the microwave can move through the food. Aim for breadth rather than depth.

☐ Ice-cream and margarine containers that are not marked as microwave safe are not suitable, as they will melt and deform at high temperatures. Also the fat in your food can absorb small quantities of toxic substances from some containers.

☐ Special microwave cookware is available. These are light and durable utensils designed so that the food will cook evenly and are the best shape for use in a microwave oven. They can be used in the freezer, taken straight from freezer to microwave, and washed in the dishwasher, but are not suitable for use in a conventional oven unless specified by the manufacturer.

☐ Cooking in a glass container will take a little longer than in microwave-safe plastic containers.

☐ Microwave-safe plastic spoons can be left in the sauce during cooking for easy stirring. Watch out for other plastic spoons that can melt into a great, colourful, plastic blob during cooking. Wooden spoons tend to leave a slightly woody taste behind.

☐ If you do not have a ring mould for cakes, make your own by putting a 10-cm diameter glass in the centre of a large, microwave-safe casserole dish.

☐ The correct microwave-safe cake pans may not need greasing. If you are cooking a heavy chocolate cake, you can use a paper towel at the bottom to absorb excess moisture.

☐ When you are in a hurry, a smaller container will speed up the cooking time.

☐ Use wood and straw dishes and paper cups, plates, towels and cartons for quick reheating.

Veal see also **Casseroles, Meat, Roasting**

☐ To **roast** veal, cook on MEDIUM-HIGH (70–80%) for 7–10 minutes per 500 g with 30 minutes' standing time in each case. Turn half-way through cooking.

☐ Slice the veal thickly to make sure that it does not toughen during cooking.

☐ Veal **stews** and **casseroles** should always be cooked on MEDIUM (50–60%), as it is a tight-fibred, lean meat, making it hard for the microwaves to pass through.

Vegetables see also individual vegetables

☐ To **steam** vegetables, cover them with a lid or plastic film and cook on HIGH (100%) for the required time. If you want to bake rather than steam them, they should be elevated on a roasting rack, or stir-fried in a browning dish.

- ☐ Do not add salt to vegetables before cooking as salt is a drying agent and will cause the vegetables to toughen. Add any salt after cooking.
- ☐ Cut vegetables into small, uniform sizes for tender, even cooking.
- ☐ When cooking vegetables use a dish that accommodates them exactly. Half-filled dishes take longer to cook.
- ☐ Always prick the skins of vegetables such as tomatoes and potatoes.
- ☐ Garden-fresh vegetables cook more quickly than those bought at the supermarket.
- ☐ Some vegetables can only be cooked once. Cabbage, Brussels sprouts and broccoli go soggy if reheated.
- ☐ Small quantities of vegetables can be **blanched** in the microwave before freezing. Place in a dish with 250–500 ml of water, cover and heat on HIGH (100%) for one-third of the usual cooking time for the vegetable. After cooking, drain and immerse the vegetables in iced water to cool them quickly, then package in the usual way for freezing. Only blanch small quantities of vegetables at a time.
- ☐ A little butter, stock or water is required when cooking soft-fibred vegetables like mushrooms.
- ☐ Since only very small amounts of water are used to cook vegetables in a microwave oven, it is not necessary to drain them before serving. Water-soluble vitamins and minerals are retained and quick cooking means less of the other nutrients are lost.

☐ Beans and carrots are hard-fibred and can become tough during cooking. Use more water than you would with other vegetables, and slice them thinly for best results.

☐ **Standing time** applies to vegetables as well as meat. Allow about 2–3 minutes for this. Always undercook vegetables so that they are still crisp and crunchy at the end of the standing time rather than shrivelled up.

☐ When cooking asparagus, broccoli and cauliflower, put the thick stems to the outside of the turntable or dish, and the flower ends in, so that they cook evenly.

☐ If cooking vegetables covered with a sauce made with eggs, cream or sour cream, cook on DEFROST (30-40%) or MEDIUM (50–60%) to prevent curdling.

☐ Don't try to can vegetables in a microwave.

☐ Overcooked vegetables can be puréed and used in soups.

☐ Stir or shake vegetables at least once during cooking.

☐ **Frozen vegetables** do not need defrosting before cooking. They can be cooked straight from the freezer, on HIGH (100%). Don't add extra water to frozen vegetables. If the vegetable is frozen in a box it is a good idea to remove the cardboard, as the dye in the box may run in the microwave, colouring the oven and the vegetable!

Vegetarians

☐ Microwave ovens are a great asset to vegetarians as microwave cooking maintains the nutrients, flavour and colour of fruit and vegetables. Furthermore they will cook vegetables to the tender but crisp stage. Vegetables are approximately 80% water and, as microwave cooking is based on the vibration of liquid molecules, little extra liquid is needed for cooking.

Volume see **Quantity**

W
~~~~~~~~~

</center>

Warming
☐ To heat your dinner plates, put a little water on each plate, or put a wet paper towel between plates, and microwave on HIGH (100%) for 20 seconds per plate. You can heat as many plates as will fit into the microwave.

Wattage
☐ Watts are a measure of electrical energy and the wattage of your microwave oven will tell you how powerful it is. A 500-watt oven will be approximately 10% slower in its cooking time than a 650-watt oven.

Wave stirrer
☐ Usually concealed in the roof of the oven, its blades disperse the microwaves. A rotating antenna performs the same function.

Whole meal cooking
☐ Ovens that offer this do not operate with a turntable. It

requires a little bit of thinking about how fast each food would cook separately. Arrange your dishes in the microwave so that the food that will require the longest cooking time is placed on the shelf, towards the right-hand side of the oven. The food in the upper right position absorbs much of the microwave energy, so any food you put straight below the shelf will take longer to cook. That's where you want to put food that will cook quickly or smaller items. Below the shelf dishes should be covered to help their contents cook more evenly and retain heat.

☐ How long to microwave this meal? Start by adding together the times it would take the items to microwave individually, including standing time, then subtract 5 minutes for the main recipe, and 2 or 3 minutes for each of the other recipes you microwave at the same time.

☐ Remember to test your food at regular intervals during the cooking time, re-arranging and removing dishes as necessary.

Wine

☐ The flavour of wine is highlighted with the short cooking time in a microwave oven, so adjust the quantity to your taste. Use only good quality wine.

Wood

☐ Wood contains moisture that will evaporate during cooking, so wooden containers may dry out and split if used for long cooking. Wood and cane containers are better for quick heating. Wooden spoons can be left in the oven for short periods of time.

☐ Check that wooden dishes or cane baskets have not been bonded with glue, staples or metal wires.

XYZ

Yams see **Sweet Potato**

Yoghurt

☐ Yoghurt will separate if overcooked, so use DEFROST (30%) where yoghurt is included in the ingredients.

Zucchini

☐ Zucchini consist of 94.6% water, so they require very little water when cooking. To cook whole zucchini, pierce the skin, add 2 tablespoons of water, cover the dish and cook on HIGH for 4–5 minutes per 500 g, stirring half-way through the cooking time. Alternatively they can be chopped, put in a plastic bag and cooked for the same time.

☐ Zucchini cakes can be made ahead and reheated. Reheat cakes on DEFROST (30–40%) for 30–40 seconds for a whole cake or about 10 seconds for individual slices. If frozen, reheat on HIGH (100%) for 15–20 seconds per slice.

☐ Zucchini bread and nutbread are delicious and attractive, easily made in the microwave and good for slicing and sandwiches.

QUICK LOOK & COOK CHART

This chart is for 600–650-watt ovens. For 500-watt ovens add 10% extra cooking time. For 800–1000-watt ovens subtract 10–15% cooking time.

FOOD	QUANTITY	DIRECTIONS	TIME
Egg SCRAMBLED	2 eggs	With a fork mix with a little milk or water and butter; mix again half-way through cooking time	2–2½ minutes on MEDIUM-HIGH (70%)
POACHED	1 egg	Break into greased custard dish or tea cup – pierce yolk – cover with plastic wrap	1 minute on MEDIUM-LOW/DEFROST (30%)
Bacon	1 rasher 2 rashers 4 rashers	Place between sheets of paper towel	1 minute on HIGH (100%) 2 minutes on HIGH (100%) 3½ minutes on HIGH (100%) (2 minutes' standing time)

FOOD	QUANTITY	DIRECTIONS	TIME
Vegetables* JACKET POTATOES	1 whole, medium size 4 whole	Wash, dry and pierce, then place directly on turntable	4 minutes on HIGH (100%) 8–10 minutes on HIGH (100%)
HARD VEGETABLES (potatoes, pumpkin, carrots, cauliflower)	500 g	Cut into small pieces, add 1 tablespoon water, cover with plastic wrap	8–10 minutes on HIGH (100%)
SOFT VEGETABLES (zucchini, mushrooms, baby squash)	500 g	Slice, sprinkle with 1 table-spoon water or a little butter, cover with plastic wrap	4–6 minutes on HIGH (100%)
FROZEN (all types)	500 g	Do not add water, cover with plastic wrap	6–8 minutes on HIGH (100%)
Fish (whole or fillets)	500 g	Cook on platter, season, dot with butter, sprinkle with lemon juice, cover with paper towel	10–12 minutes on MEDIUM (50%)

*Note: Use a wide, shallow, round dish for best results when cooking vegetables. Add seasonings to vegetables after cooking

FOOD	QUANTITY	DIRECTIONS	TIME
Meat			
ROASTS (beef, lamb, pork, veal)	per 500 g	Place fat side down on a rack, cover with paper towel, turn half-way through cooking time	12–15 minutes on MEDIUM (50%)
Poultry			
CHICKEN (whole or pieces)	per 500 g	Place on a rack or in baking dish, cover with paper towel, turn half-way through cooking time	10 minutes per 500 g on MEDIUM-HIGH (70%)
TURKEY (whole)	per 500 g	As for chicken	15–18 minutes per 500 g on MEDIUM (50%)
Reheating			
MEAT PIES (fresh)	1 individual	Wrap in paper towel, place upside down in oven	1½–2 minutes on MEDIUM-HIGH (70%)
	2 individual		3½ minutes on MEDIUM-HIGH (70%)
(frozen)	1 individual		5–7 minutes on DEFROST (30%), then 2 minutes on MEDIUM-HIGH (70%)

FOOD	QUANTITY	DIRECTIONS	TIME
APPLE PIES (fresh)	1 small individual or slice	Place on serving plate between paper towel	1½ minutes on MEDIUM-HIGH (70%)
PIZZA (frozen)	1 large	Remove foil tray, place on several sheets of paper towel (will be very soft)	7 minutes on DEFROST (30%), then 7 minutes on MEDIUM-HIGH (70%)
INDIVIDUAL MEALS (fresh)	1 serve	Cover with plastic wrap	2 minutes on MEDIUM-HIGH (70%)
(frozen)	1 serve		7 minutes on DEFROST (30%), then 3–5 minutes on MEDIUM (50%)
FRANKFURTERS	1	Place in oven on paper towel, pierce skin	1 minute on MEDIUM-HIGH (70%)
	2		1½ minutes on MEDIUM-HIGH (70%)
BREAD ROLLS	1	Place in oven	10 seconds on HIGH (100%)
	2		15–20 seconds on HIGH (100%)